IMAGES
of America

WHEATON

The most memorable piece of playground equipment in the Adventure Playground at Wheaton Regional Park was the decommissioned military jet. The jet was not an F-4 Phantom (the jet in the news of that era) as children imagined but a F7U Cutlass, a U.S. Navy–based fighter-bomber of the early cold war era. It was a highly unusual, semi-tailless design. Although a first in many forms of engineering, the plane was deemed so unsafe that they were decommissioned and many ended up in playgrounds across the country. This one arrived in the summer of 1962. There were stairs into the cockpit and a sliding board out the other side. Another was installed at Cabin John Park. Nearby the unique slide/jet were Cinderella's carriage, real farm animals on Old MacDonald's Farm, and a miniature train. The Shorefield Picnic and Playground is still at the park entrance at Shorefield Road off Georgia Avenue and part of the original installation—the miniature train still runs from its station. (WKCC.)

ON THE COVER: During construction of the WJSV (WTOP) transmitter building, this work crew photograph was taken on December 18, 1939. Everyone involved with the project felt he or she were making history and wanted the record to last the ages. Most (if not all) of the early WJSV photographs were the work of Theodor Horydczak, a Washington photographer who documented the architecture and social life of the Washington metropolitan area from 1920 to 1940. (Bonneville International.)

IMAGES
of America

WHEATON

Laura-Leigh Palmer

ARCADIA
PUBLISHING

Published by Arcadia Publishing
Charleston, South Carolina

Library of Congress Catalog Card Number: 2008939477

For all general information contact Arcadia Publishing at:
Telephone 843-853-2070
Fax 843-853-0044
E-mail sales@arcadiapublishing.com
For customer service and orders:
Toll-Free 1-888-313-2665

Visit us on the Internet at www.arcadiapublishing.com

*To all those who believe that mankind will come to know
good and that knowledge is something to be shared.*

CONTENTS

ACKNOWLEDGMENTS

Wheaton is rich in history but has no historical society. The information used to create this book is from members of the community. The best thanks I can give is to make sure that what was gathered is available to others in the future. This is a community treasure that needs to find a permanent home.

I apologize to all those I promised to contact or call on again but did not. Many stories are also missing. For those who have a Wheaton story to tell, I can be reached by e-mail at laura.leigh@ asapgraphics.com. This book is a beginning, not an ending.

My deepest gratitude to those collectors before me—Chuck Boynton, Rev. B. Ross Morrison, Granville Klink, and Carol Piper—and to those who allowed access to their efforts: Vicky Surles and Tim Wiens of the Wheaton and Kensington Chamber of Commerce; Rev. Larry White and Marie Satterwhite of First Baptist Church of Wheaton; Carol Piper (before her second retirement), Hilary Strycker (archives), and Edith Michel (division chief) of the Maryland-National Capital Park and Planning Commission; and Ken Sleeman (transmitter site manager), Bonneville International.

Thanks to Walter and Carol Petzold, the Bobrow and Skaggs families, Leonard A. Becraft, Joan Gartrell (Hughes Methodist Church), all the radio guys, and Bob Murch (williamfuld.com). Thanks to Jim Knowles (Knowles Printing) for finding out just what type of jet was in Wheaton Regional Park at the eleventh hour.

Special thanks to Evelyn and Seward Horad, who opened their home to my mobile collecting station (iPod, iBook, and portable scanner) at odd hours of the day and night and also made sure I was fed and watered. Also a special thanks to Mary Hertel, who, besides allowing me to invade her home, has been a willing tour guide as we drove through the community, diligent in researching questions I come up with and also (with grave reservations) letting me borrow her books.

I surely would have given up this task without Kathleen Thompson, who knows who (and how) to contact, and most importantly her impatience that the work wasn't done.

Photograph abbreviations:

Author	Laura-Leigh Palmer
FBCW	First Baptist Church of Wheaton
LOC-GMDW	Library of Congress, Geography and Map Division, Washington
LOC-PPDW	Library of Congress, Prints and Photographs Division, Washington
MCHS	Montgomery County Historical Society
M-NCPPC	Maryland-National Capital Park and Planning Commission
MSALR	Maryland State Archives Land Records
WKCC	Wheaton and Kensington Chamber of Commerce

INTRODUCTION

Wheaton (like many Montgomery County communities) has no official boundaries—the name was first used in 1869 for the post office. This post office closed in 1906, but the name remained as a place of residence in the U.S. Census and to designate a large election district. Unincorporated areas are hard to define in exact terms. Boundaries in this book are from records of residency (the Wheaton census prior to World War II and land records) and interviews of people in the community. This makes Wheaton the sum of zip codes 20902 and 20906 (Silver Spring) and parts of 20895 (outside the town of Kensington) and sections of 20853 (Rockville). Despite a lack of "official status," many believe there is a Wheaton no matter where the U.S. Postal Service or U.S. Census now designates their home as residing.

The greater part of Wheaton's European settlement started with two tracts of land east of Rock Creek patented by Col. William Joseph in 1689, the 3,860 acres called Hermitage, and parts of the Joseph's Park tract of 4,220 acres. Colonel Joseph never lived on his land but gave it to his son, who sold it in 1705 for 500 pounds. The area was still Prince George's County. Prior to the arrival of the Europeans, the area was home to the Piscataway Indians.

Most early landowners rented their land, requiring their tenants to pay with a portion of the crop and improve the property with orchards and dwellings. By 1776, enough people had settled the area that Montgomery County came into its own. The banks of the Northwest Branch to the west and Rock Creek to the east, with Norbeck in the north as the upper limits, began to define the community. Tobacco was the earliest crop and was exported to European markets, but as the soil was depleted, production shifted to wheat. The introduction of scientific farming methods and lime brought in by rail helped bring back the soil from its years growing tobacco. In the 1920s, farms were primarily dairy and produce, which negated the need for heavy fertilization, and most of the production was sold locally.

In 1797, Robert Brown began acquiring property and purchased part of the Hermitage tract. He had arrived in 1761 from Ireland as a skilled stonemason and worked on both the President's House (White House) and the Capitol. His son, also named Robert Brown, negotiated a deal for the Hermitage land after his father's death and added to the holdings. The Agricultural Censure in 1850 listed these as 230 acres of improved land, 1,170 acres unimproved, with 7 horses, 16 milch cows, 5 working oxen, 40 sheep, and 16 swine. The farm produced 500 bushels of wheat, 400 bushels of Indian corn, 60 pounds of wool, 7 tons of hay, 300 pounds of butter, and no tobacco. According to the list of "Slave Inhabitants" that year, he had eight slaves. His land went from what is now Wheaton and Kensington south to Forest Glen and from Georgia Avenue west to Rock Creek. He owned a large portion within these boundaries but not all, since many landowners would not sell. As Robert Brown's children married, the land was divided among them, their spouses, and their children.

At the cross section of three roads that cut through the farmland, a small business area developed. The north/south road was Brookeville Pike (Georgia Avenue), a toll road from Washington City

(District of Columbia) to Brookeville, Maryland, and beyond to Baltimore. It was improved with gravel, stone, and oyster shells. Veirs Mill Road, also called the Rockville-Washington Road, was a coach road, and parts of it were a plank road (made from split logs laid side by side) from Wheaton to Rockville and leading to ferry crossings on the Potomac and to Point of Rocks, connecting with Northern Virginia. The third main road was Bladensburg Road (University Boulevard), also known later as the Kensington-Wheaton Road and the Wheaton–Four Corners Road. It connected the communities of Georgetown, Bethesda, Chevy Chase, and Bladensburg.

On February 2, 1826, the first recorded name for the area, Leesborough, is listed in U.S. Post Office records. Over the following 37 years, Leesborough lost the post office twice. In 1845–1849, it was named Hermitage and possibly relocated to the estate of that same name (built by the Bowies in 1748–1749) or another older building near the estate, also called Hermitage, located at Union Pike (Georgia Avenue) and Layhill Road.

"Mitchells X Roads" (Wheaton) is marked on maps in the 1860s as the intersection of Old Bladensburg Road (University Boulevard) and the Union Turnpike (Georgia Avenue). The name refers to Mitchell's Tavern (destroyed by fire in 1940), owned and operated by Richard T. Mitchell. It stood on the northeast corner of Georgia Avenue and University Boulevard and was reported to have been well over 100 years old in 1865. It was supposed to have been "out of bounds" for Union soldiers during the Civil War because of its "over flowing" bar. During this time, maps and correspondence refer to the area as Leesboro. Nearby a tollgate stood for the turnpike, and an ordinary (inn) was at the junction of the Rockville-Washington (Veirs Mill) Road and Seventh Street Pike (Georgia Avenue). At least two blacksmith shops serviced the "best roads in the county" that made up the crossroads.

On October 5, 1869, George Plyer became postmaster and named the post office Wheaton. Plyer was one of the new residents who came to the area after having served in the Civil War. As a private in 1861 of K Company, 36th Infantry (New York) of the Union army, George Plyer and his unit came to the nation's capital. The unit's first duty was the construction of Fort Massachusetts (the unofficial name given by the soldiers), later named Fort Stevens in memory of Brig. Gen. Isaac Ingalls Stevens after his death in 1862 at the Battle of Chantilly (or Ox Hill).

Fort Stevens, located approximately 6 miles south of Leesboro (Wheaton), was one of the ring forts built to protect Washington, D.C., during the Civil War. It was from there on July 11–12, 1864, that Gen. Frank Wheaton, Union army, successfully defended Washington, D.C., against Gen. Jubal Early's Confederate army. The Confederates passed though Rockville, Leesboro (Wheaton), and Silver Spring, retreating the same way. It was the only major Civil War military engagement within the District of Columbia and was the second time a sitting president, Abraham Lincoln at the time, came under enemy fire. The first was James Madison when he went to Bladensburg in 1814 when the British invaded Washington D.C., in the War of 1812.

Before this battle, both George Plyer and his good friend 1st Lt. Charles Eccleston had returned to the area after they were mustered out of the service in July 1863. They both served in the 36th Infantry, enlisting at the same time, but served in different companies of the 36th for most of the war. It is highly likely they were at the fort when the battle occurred. Many of the locals joined the army of their preference during the engagement, and they both said Wheaton had been their commander. As a result of the battle, General Wheaton became a folk hero and the post office was named in his honor.

Not everyone agreed with the new name for the area. In 1874, Henrietta E. Tetly (no doubt a longtime resident) became postmistress and returned the name to Leesboro. A year later, Wheaton was reinstated when George Plyer was reappointed postmaster. The Wheaton Post Office remained on his property at the corner of Plyers Mill and Brookeville Pike (Georgia Avenue) until in 1890 the Plyer Post Office was established.

The Wheaton Post Office moved to Mitchell's Crossroads in 1890, and G. O. B. (Georgium Osborne B.) Cissell, who now owned the tavern, was named postmaster. He was from Howard County and had married Catherine A. Stubbs on January 31, 1883. According to family lore,

Catherine's grandfather William Edward Stubbs used to play poker with President Buchanan and Secretary of War Edwin M. Stanton. William also at one time owned Lafayette Square in Washington—all of the houses on the block. The Cissell family grew, and the tavern became the primary family residence. He opened a store across the road. In 1906, the Wheaton Post Office was the last of the many local post offices to close because of a drop of population in the entire county. Mail was sent to Sandy Spring.

With the passage of the Civil Service Act of 1883, new arrivals in the lower part of the county made up for lost farmers and began a suburb for a stable governmental work force of civil servants. Unlike many areas of the United States, the suburban population around Washington, D.C., was primarily composed of the middle class from the beginning. Wheaton, without a commuter service, grew more slowly than Kensington, which had lines for both train and trolley. By 1920, among the regularly scheduled trains were 18 per day that were devoted just to carrying passengers.

The growing government workforce gave a ready market for local dairy and produce, but the value of the land was greater than its value as farmland. Planning began in the 1890s for subdivisions, but the area remained predominantly farmland and large estates for several more decades. Population pressure along the rail lines (Kensington, Garrett Park, and the like) strained both water and sewage facilities. An outbreak of typhoid in 1898 and the pollution of Rock Creek were issues that created in 1912 the Washington Suburban Sanitary Commission (WSSC). The decisions of the WSSC went far in determining what areas would be developed in the years to come.

People who moved to Wheaton wished to be "out in the country," and with the invention of the automobile and the existing roads, they were the pioneer commuters. Horses trained and raced on many properties, and fox hunting was still a major pastime. As the population grew, the paying of tolls became a "thorn in the flesh to the patrons of the roads," and the taxpayers of "Wheaton, Colesville and Olney Districts in which these roads live" petitioned the county commissioners to ask the Good Roads Commission to take "as a gift the Union and the Washington, Colesville and Ashton Turnpikes to improve and maintain them." Actually the three local districts bought the roads with a special bond issue and an increase in property taxes for the interest on the bonds. The roads were eventually purchased in 1913 for $1,000 a mile. For the Union Turnpike (Georgia Avenue), the total was $25,000 and the state took over maintenance.

Dramatic change occurred to the landscape of the area after World War II. During the war, only about 29,000 people were living in Wheaton, mostly on farms and large estates. The population doubled from 1940 to 1950 and then doubled again from 1950 to 1960. A massive influx of federal government workers to the area during the war created a huge housing shortage; after the war, these people remained along with returning veterans who made the area their home. Building could not keep pace with demand. With the new arrivals came new schools, new churches, new businesses, and new roads. Most commuted to jobs in Washington, D.C., while living and raising their families in the community. People whose families had been in the area for generations lived in subdivisions on land that only a generation ago their parents and grandparents had farmed.

All this change was rapid. In 1945, Springbrook Forest, developed by George Moss, in Kemp Mill advertised for families to create homes "somewhere out in the country." The property that had been the Gilmore Mica Mine was an entirely different subdivision from the speculative offering of many completed houses on smaller lots that came to dominate the metropolitan area. Viers Mill Village in 1948 was the second mass suburban development (Twinbrook in Rockville built in 1947 was the first), and the houses seemed to appear as if "built over night." Builders concentrated on how fast they could put up homes, and little was preserved as mass production housing went up in some cases at a pace of 10 houses a day. A few older homes still exist, but most are entirely hemmed in among the post–World War II developments.

With this growing population, in 1949, the U.S. Postal Service opened a branch of Silver Spring—Wheaton Station on Amherst Avenue. Many other communities had their identity absorbed into the Silver Spring postal designation in a geographic area slightly smaller than Baltimore. The community, not happy with this loss of identity, petitioned and succeeded in

1965 (after many years of protests) in gaining permission for residents to use "Wheaton, MD" for zip codes 20902 and 20906. The Wheaton and Kensington Chamber of Commerce did much to gain this permission, with the belief that a community identity was needed to ensure needed services and planning for the influx of the residents of Wheaton.

One of the biggest needs became roads, which had become impassable. The "Avenue of Progress" (Georgia Avenue) was widened from two lanes to six, and the dedication on November 1, 1952, was celebrated with a parade and ribbon cutting by Governor McKeldin. Wheaton advertised itself as the "Community of Tomorrow—Today." More changes were to come, and the building continued.

If it had not ended before, by 1954, the idea of Wheaton being in the country ended forever. Work began on 800 houses on a 500-acre wooded tract called Kemp Mill Estates (Kay Construction Company), and addresses that had been on Kemp Mill Road disappeared and reappeared on the newly named Arcola Avenue. That same year, approval was granted for the development of the Heitmuller tract, which opened as Wheaton Plaza (Westfield Wheaton) in 1959. Besides homes, a building boom for needed schools, fire stations, libraries, community centers, churches, shopping areas, and parks enveloped the area. In 1958, the Maryland-National Capital Park and Planning Commission began buying land to create Wheaton Regional Park. These 536 acres became a refuge and sanctuary to many in the community as green space disappeared.

The pictorial history that follows shows Wheaton as it evolved and records the lives of only a few who made this place their home, places that are now gone, and some that have remained. It is a collection of people—farmers, government workers, horse racers, inventors, builders, business owners, and volunteers—who built this community. It is far from a complete history of the area, but it is a beginning.

One

COMMUNITY BEGINNINGS

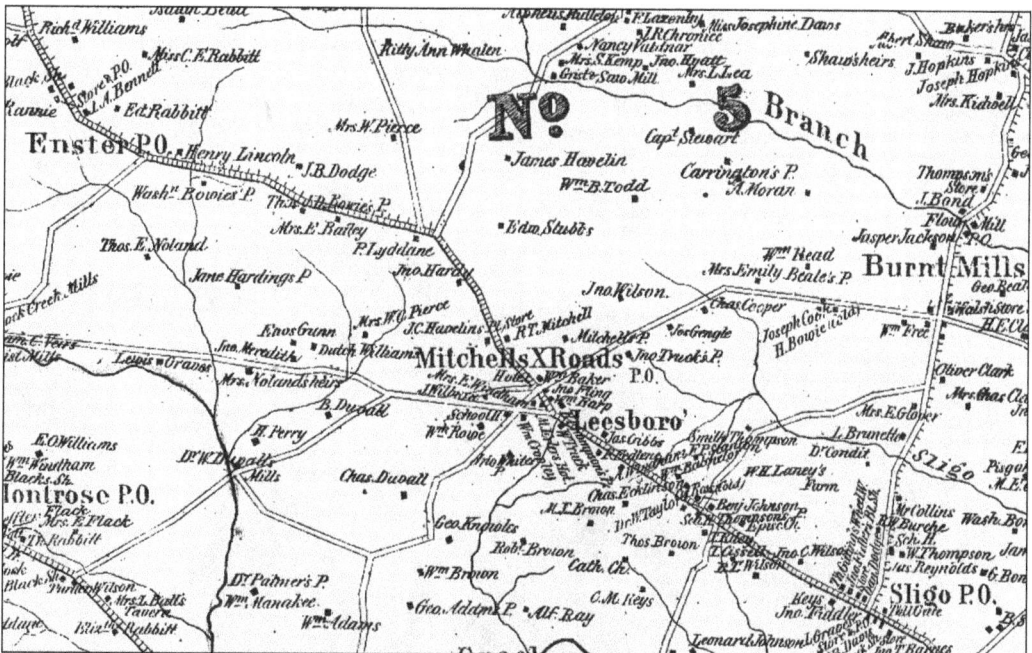

Martenet and Bond's 1865 Map of Montgomery County shows the early names that have faded from public memory: Mitchells X Roads, Leesboro, and Enster. Wheaton triangle is formed with the convergence of the crossroads: the Seventh Street Pike (Georgia Avenue), marked as a toll road; the Rockville-Washington Road (Veirs Mill Road); and Bladensburg Road (University Boulevard). (LOC-GMDW.)

Early structures still exist in Wheaton, but layers of remodeling hide many. This log cabin came to light in 1966 as the First Baptist Church of Wheaton began work on a new annex. Their original chapel, the "Old Brown House," had survived demolition in 1927 when the Maryland State Roads Commission straightened Brookeville Pike (Georgia Avenue). The structure was moved back—west and south—some 90 feet, turned, and placed on a new foundation with no harm except a few cracks in the plaster. It stood for another 39 years. The c. 1816 Old Brown House, with logs measuring 12 inches thick, 20 inches wide, and 24 feet long, was one of two possible structures shown on early maps as an ordinary (a term used at that time to describe a place with overnight accommodations, such as an inn or tavern). (Both photographs by Rev. B. Ross Morrison, FBCW.)

The Mitchell house (lower right) in 1953 has a clear view of the WSSC water tanks. In 1864, Richard T. Mitchell, whose hotel-tavern was in the "primary trade area" of Mitchell's X Roads, had parts of the Hermitage track resurveyed and probably at that time acquired this property. The road running horizontally is University Boulevard. Note the residential Wheaton Triangle area. (M-NCPPC.)

In 1865, the population of Mitchell's Crossroads did not exceed 200, including men, women, and children. Since that time, a house belonging to the Mitchells has existed in this location, appearing on the atlases and in land records. This home may have been rebuilt at some time. It stands amid a post–World War II development. (Author.)

Edward Stubbs, an official with the U.S. Department of State, purchased Shorefield in 1841 as a summer home. During the Civil War, the renamed Avon became the primary residence of the family until the 1930s. The name of the house may be a reference to the valley of the Avon in Steuben County, New York, a previous Stubbs residence. It became a part of Wheaton Regional Park in 1959. (M-NCPPC.)

John Hardy built three homes on his farm. The family home, Mount Calvert, is the only one that remains, notable in its day for its fireplaces and boxwoods. It later became the Kingswell Estate and is listed in land records as being built in 1853. Although listed in good condition, the property was recommended for removal in 1979 from the Index of Historic Sites in Montgomery County. (Author.)

The original frontage of the Hardy farm ran from Randolph Road to Parker Avenue, and in 1954, some of the property was retained. Many people tried to remain and farm part of their land during the World War II building boom, and these strip farms were not an uncommon site in the early 1950s. Some families developed the land themselves at a later date or sold the property to later developers. The Hardys had been landowners in the area for generations and farmed their own land. They would never own slaves; in order to get laborers, they hired them from the slave owners in the neighborhood. Mary Hardy, in 1898, gave a name to a new post office at Georgia Avenue and Randolph Road—Glenmont. It was only open three years, but the name for the neighborhood remains. (M-NCPPC.)

Walter Magruder later owned part of Shorefield, and his house was the birthplace of numerous children. His daughter Duane married Charles D. Stubbs (a great-grandson of Edward Stubbs). The Magruder family posed in the 1960s at the homestead now located behind the miniature train at Wheaton Regional Park. From left to right are (first row) Val and Barbara (Hicks) Vercumba, Bobby Owens, Millie (Davis) Conroy, Bette (Davis) and Bob Jarnagin, Pat Owens (Mrs. Kenny Owens), Wilbur D. Stubbs II, Kenny Owens, Ted Swaim (married Beverly Hicks), Jim Owens, and Ronnie Specht (married Beverly Magruder); (second row) Mary Lou and Gene Magruder Jr., Pat (Magruder) and Sonny Griffin, Jimmy and Elaine (Magruder) Jones, Kay (Magruder) Lyttle, Beverly (Hicks) Swaim, and Bobby Magruder Jr.; (third row) Duane Grace Magruder Stubbs, Charles D. Stubbs, Daisy Elizabeth Magruder, Eva-Lea Magruder, Hilda Case Magruder Davis, Evelyn Fox (Mrs. Bobby Magruder Jr.), Robert ("Bobbie") Magruder, Ella Minerva Magruder Hale, Betty (Hayden) Magruder, Corrie Edna Magruder, Helen Marie Magruder Hicks, Hanson Hicks, Mamie Ida Magruder Owens, Earl Owens, L. Clifton Magruder, and Danny Hale. (Christopher M. Stubbs.)

Two

THE CIVIL WAR ERA

George Plyer, age 24, on May 13, 1861, enlisted as a Union private in Company K, 36th Infantry (New York). He mustered out July 15, 1863. The 36th (Washington Volunteers) from July 1861 until March 1862 were stationed at the capital. Their first camp was Meridian Hill with Couch's Brigade. Their first task was construction of Fort Massachusetts (officially Fort Stevens). (LOC-PPDW.)

In July 1864, Confederate lieutenant general Jubal Early's army marched to Washington, D.C. They were delayed a full day by Gen. Lew Wallace's small force at Monocacy. Along Union Turnpike (Georgia Avenue), Martha Brown (Mrs. Eccleston) remembered the soldiers spearing the family poultry with bayonets and cooking them over campfires. The Confederates camped at and spared the Batchelor house (site of St. John's Catholic Church) but burned the home belonging to the Brown family. (LOC-PPDW.)

On July 11, 1864, the Confederates reached the outskirts of Washington near Silver Spring, and skirmishers advanced to test the forces at Fort Stevens. It was manned only by Home Guards with an extemporized force of clerks, veterans, and convalescent troops. At noon, Wheaton and his troops "after being rushed by water," according to Vol. 20, Dictionary of American Biography, 1930, arrived at the pier and began their march up the Seventh Street Pike (Georgia Avenue). (LOC-PPDW.)

Gen. Frank Wheaton was born in Providence, Rhode Island. He was a first lieutenant in the 1st U.S. Cavalry on the Native American frontier when the Civil War began. In 1861, as lieutenant colonel of the 2nd Rhode Island Infantry, he took command at the First Battle of Bull Run and was promoted to colonel. As brigadier general of volunteers in 1862, he commanded the 3rd Brigade, 3rd Division, Sixth Army Corps (the VI Corps) and led them in heavy fighting at the Battle of Chancellorsville and limited action at the Battle of Gettysburg. He remained in command during Grant's Overland Campaign in 1864 and during the Siege of Petersburg. After Wheaton was promoted to command of a division, his men were hurried to Washington, D.C., to help repel Jubal Early's raid on the capital. Wheaton earned the brevet rank of major general in both the volunteer and regular services. In 1873, he commanded the expedition against Modoc Indians in California. Wheaton was appointed colonel of the 2nd U.S. Infantry in 1874, promoted to brigadier general in 1892, and major general in 1897. He retired from the army in 1897. (LOC-PPDW.)

THE REBEL ATTACK ON WASHINGTON, D.C.

By Gen. JUBAL A. EARLY. Confederate Army.

PLAN OF THE REBEL ATTACK ON WASHINGTON, D.C. JULY 11th and 12th 1864.
Maj Genl H.G. Wright. Union Forces 20,000 — Rebel Force 12000 under Genl Early & Breckinridge

Union Loss 140 Killed 220 wounded. Rebels unknown.

Union forces Infantry — Cavalry ███ Artillery Batteries ††† — Rebel Forces - Infantry — Cavalry ███ Guns †

Copy of Official Plan made in the Office of Col Alexander, U.S.A. Chief
Engineer of The Defenses of
Washington.

by R.K. Sneden, Topg Engr. U.S.A.
Sept 1864.

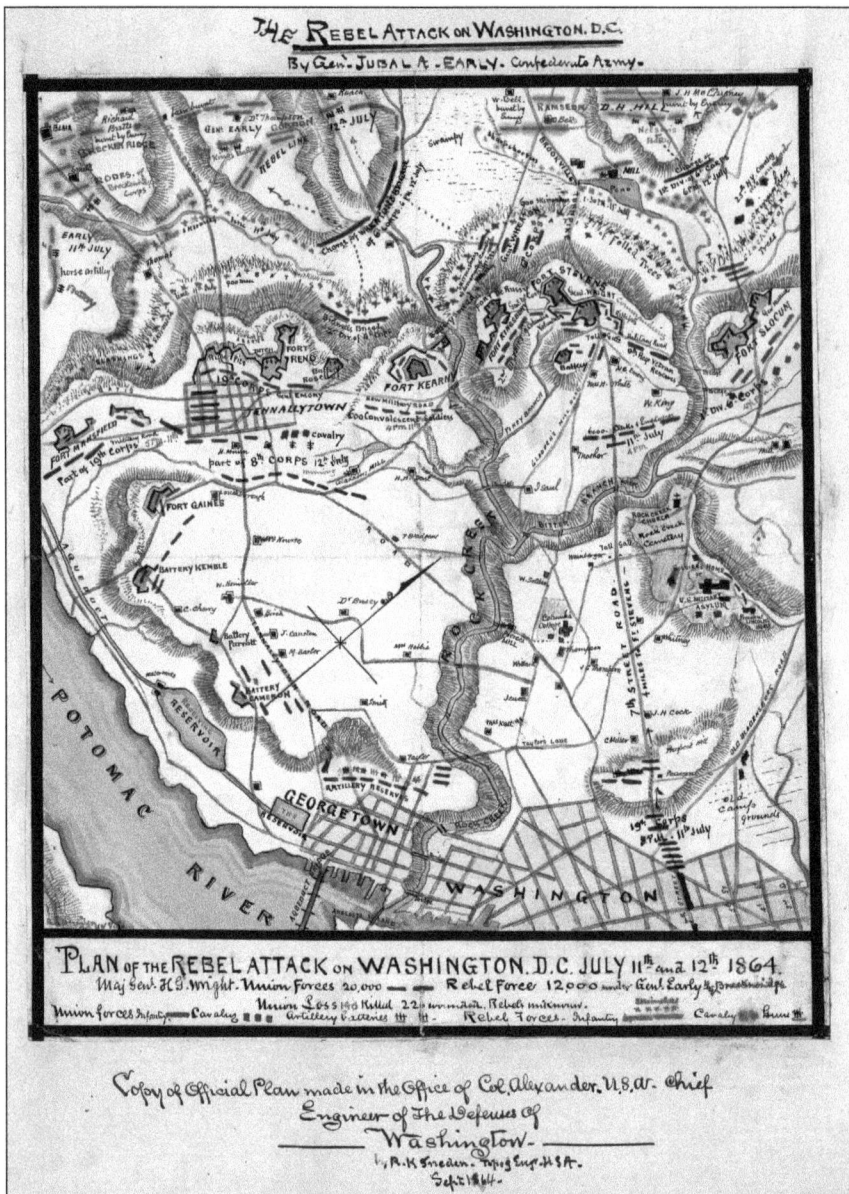

On July 12, the Confederates began an attack but were repulsed by the veteran Union troops that had arrived during the night. VI Corps drove the Confederate skirmishers back from their advanced positions in front of Fort Stevens. A Confederate sharpshooter narrowly missed President Lincoln, who was watching the battle. Maj. Gen. Horatio Wright (U.S. Army) sent out a force led by Col. Daniel Bidwell's brigade of Brig. Gen. Frank Wheaton's 2nd Division, VI Corps, to push back the sharpshooters. A firefight ensued, with casualties of 38 percent in Bidwell's regiments. The Union defenders held, and Early's sharpshooters receded into their lines. Recognizing that veterans now defended the Union capital, Early abandoned any thought of taking the city. Withdrawing during the night, the Confederates marched toward White's Ford on the Potomac, ending the invasion of Maryland. "We didn't take Washington," Early told his staff officers, "but we scared Abe Lincoln like Hell." The troops passed through Leesboro (Wheaton) again during their retreat. (LOC-GMDW.)

Two men in 1917 are reading the plaque at Fort Stevens that marks the spot where President Lincoln narrowly missed death when a Confederate sharpshooter hit assistant surgeon Cornelius Crawford of the 102nd Pennsylvania, who was at Lincoln's side on July 12, 1864. The war's top generals were missing that day, but the fighting outside Washington could be considered some of the most critical of the war. The raid nearly captured the nation's capital and almost killed Lincoln. Had either event occurred during the summer (a critical presidential election year), Lincoln's sitting vice president, Hannibal Hamlin of Maine, and not his running mate Andrew Johnson would have succeeded him. Lincoln in June 1864 had been nominated not as a Republican but on a Union ticket. The North remained unsure of the war's outcome. What would have happened if Lincoln had died that day? The memorial and remnants of Fort Stevens are located 6 miles south of Wheaton off Georgia Avenue at Thirteenth and Quackenbos Streets NW. (LOC-PPDW.)

On July 13, 1904, a monument was dedicated at Battleground National Cemetery (near Fort Stevens) that marks the grave of 41 Union soldiers who died in the Battle of Fort Stevens. Part of the inscription reads, "To the gallant sons of Onondaga County, NY who fought on this field July 12, 1864, in defense of Washington and in the presence of Abraham Lincoln." (LOC-PPDW.)

At the time of the battle, Grace Episcopal Church (replaced in 1896 after a fire) was on Brookeville Pike (Georgia Avenue). After the Battle of Fort Stevens, a mass grave site was placed in the church graveyard for 17 unknown Confederate dead. A shaft, made of granite, marks the grave. A new trolley line on Georgia Avenue forced the movement of the Confederate graves to their present location. (Author.)

"GEN. WHEATON IS DEAD—Won His Rank Through Bravery in Battle" started his *Washington Post* obituary. He died in his home in Washington, D.C., on June 18, 1903. The funeral started with a simple service, then a "ritualistic service of the Episcopal Church at St. Johns with the Right Reverend Henry Y. Satterlee, Bishop of Washington." The Engineers' Band led the military escort to Section 1 of Arlington Cemetery. The firing of a major general's salute, 13 guns, by the artillery concluded the service. A year later, 1st Lt. Frank Wheaton Rowel (Wheaton's grandson) unveiled the monument the state of Rhode Island dedicated to its native son: "I have finished my course, I have fought the fight, I have kept the faith." Currently the opposite side is missing the bronze portrait of General Wheaton provided by his widow. (Both author.)

Maj. Gen. George Washington Getty (U.S. Army) was born in Georgetown, D.C., on October 2, 1819. He graduated from West Point in 1840. A living memorial has been created in Wheaton, a small pocket park, named after him on land he bought in 1882—the Batchelor Farm where the Confederates camped in 1864. He retired there in 1883 with his wife and seven children. He died in 1901. (LOC-PPDW.)

Getty fought in the Peninsula campaign, South Mountain, Antietam, Fredericksburg, Suffolk, Wilderness, Petersburg (and the same day made brevet brigadier general and brevet major general), and the Shenandoah Valley campaign. He was a colonel after the war. He was not present at Fort Stevens in 1864, it is assumed because of severe wounds from the Battle in the Wilderness. He and his wife, Elizabeth Graham Stevenson, are buried in Arlington Cemetery in Section 1. (Author.)

Three

"BEST ROADS" BRING
NEW ARRIVALS

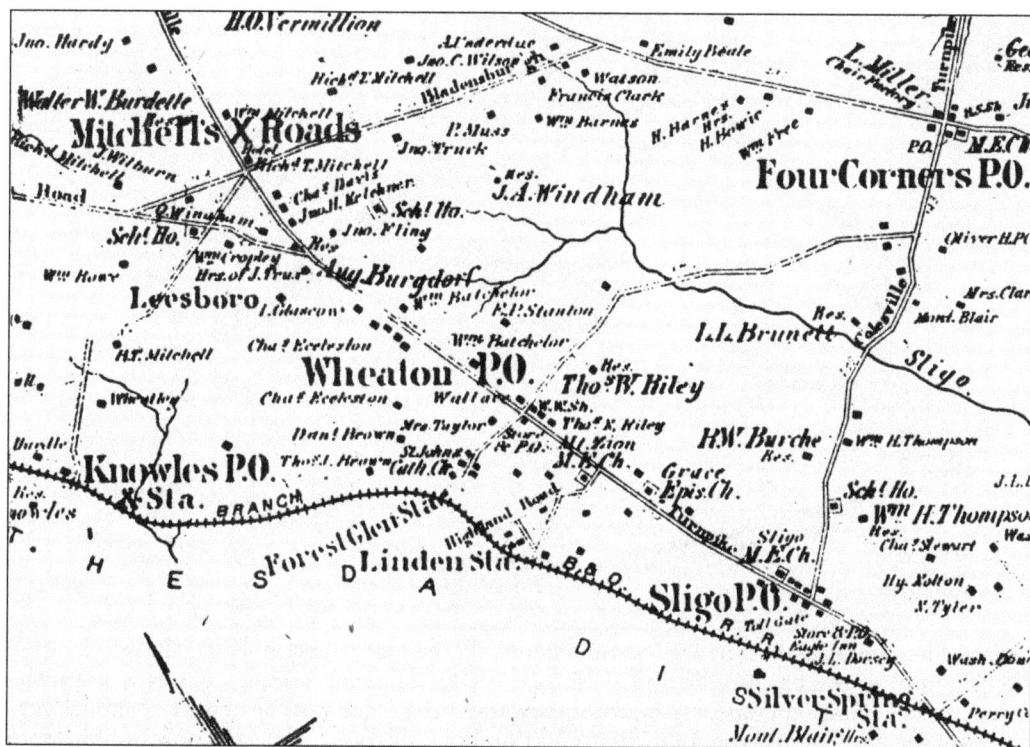

Mitchell's Cross Roads is still on the map, but the name Wheaton appears—as entered according to an act of Congress in the year 1878 by G. M. Hopkins, in the office of the Librarian of Congress in Washington. The Wheaton Post Office, however, is near Forest Glen Road and not where any past written or oral histories indicate. (WKCC.)

Col. Charles Eccleston encouraged his friend George Plyer to live in Leesboro (soon to be Wheaton). Plyer bought one of the oldest homes (100 years at that time) along with 25 acres. Plyer became postmaster on October 5, 1869, and would build a store on the property that included the Wheaton Post Office. The house in 1948 was Hughes Methodist's first parsonage and almost their Sunday school. (Hughes Methodist Church.)

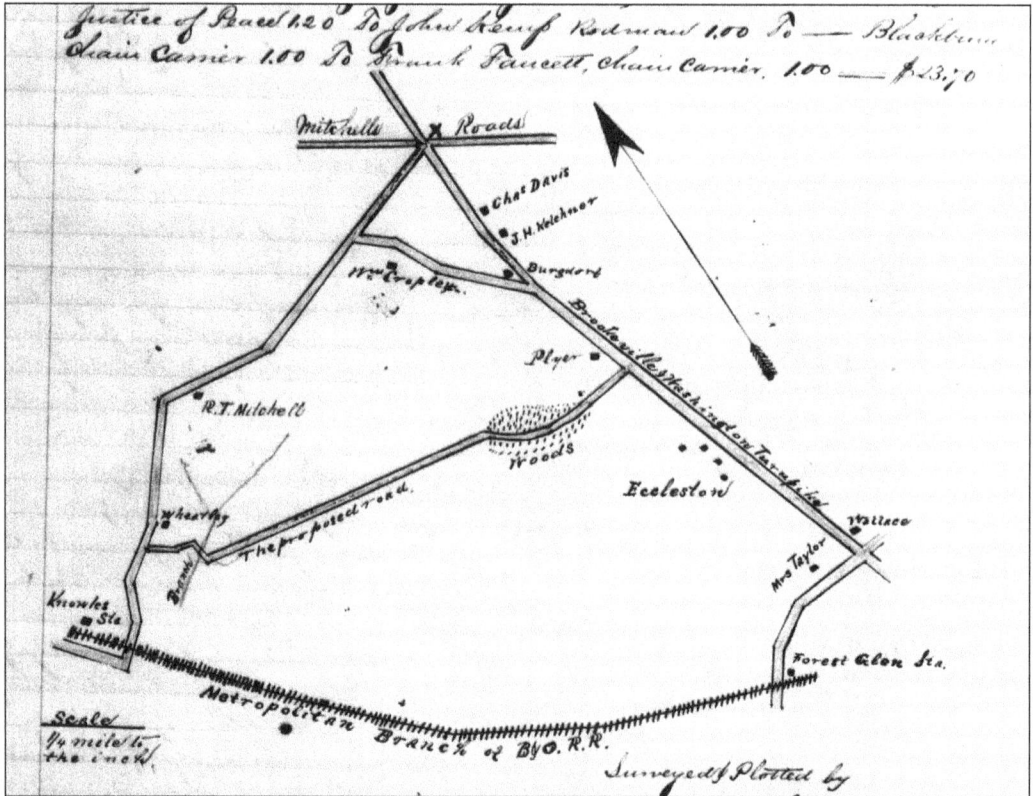

George Plyer and neighbors in 1882 wanted to rebuild the road that connected Knowles Station (Kensington) to the Brookeville and Washington Pike (Georgia Avenue). Roads were private concerns, but county commissioners sent surveyors. At the request of the county commissioners for Montgomery County, the following report and plat of the road from Knowles Station to Brookeville and Washington Pike petitioned for by B. G. Duvall, George Plyer, Mrs. Knowles, and William Wheatley was recorded February 6, 1883. The report stated, "Present county road (Plyer's Mill Road) from old cherry tree to the Bladensburg and Hughes Bridge road has been created more than forty years and is now grown up." (MSALR.)

The Haviland mystery began on December 24, 1885, when a driverless team of horses was abandoned at a store on the Brookeville-Washington Pike (Georgia Avenue) in the vicinity of the "Wheaton Post Office." Philip Haviland, the miller at Muncaster Mill, had gone into the city with a mill spindle to be repaired, staying overnight to wait for the repair. His disappearance during his return created much speculation. Theories were that he had run away because of debt, committed suicide, or was murdered. Murdered was the most popular guess. W. E. Muncaster, his landlord, dispelled theories about debt and suicide. Haviland was losing the mill lease, but Muncaster said, "It was simply a business transaction and led to no unpleasantness between us." Haviland did not have enough capital to run the mill at full capacity. A convict 26 years later made a deathbed confession that he and a friend meant to rob Haviland but accidentally killed him with a blow to the head. They sank the body in Rock Creek not far away. (LOC-PPDW.)

Allen Bowie Davis and his heirs were instrumental in the construction and operation of the roads that carried travelers through Wheaton in the 19th century. Westminster Road (Georgia Avenue) was scarcely passable in the best of weather. Davis formed the Brookeville and Washington Turnpike Company in 1830 to open produce markets in the city. Not until 1850 did work begin with the newly incorporated Union Plank and Turnpike Company. Davis was president, and his nephew Col. Washington Bowie III (left) was an early secretary-treasurer; his son Washington Bowie IV (right) provided legal counsel. Another son, Donald Bowie, recalled in 1952 the early days when, at the age of 12, he helped with the company's books. "Colonel" was an honorary title bestowed on Washington Bowie III (too young for the Civil War) by Civil War veterans entertained in his homes at Roseneath and Hermitage in Montgomery County. Colonel Bowie had many business ventures, an intriguing one being the Kennard Novelty Company, which manufactured the Ouija board from 1890–1892. (Robert Murch, williamfuld.com.)

Washington Bowie IV (known as "Junior") was born November 20, 1872, on the family's Roseneath estate in Montgomery County, the third child of Col. Washington Bowie III and Nettie Schley. His military career started in 1894 as a private, and in 1934, he was promoted to brigadier general. He had a law practice as well as a 52-year career with the Fidelity and Deposit Company in Baltimore. (LOC-PPDW.)

Junior's most well-known client during his law career was William Fuld, his father's good friend and inventor of the Ouija board. Junior became known as the "Great Ouija Defender," always working pro bono for the cause. His children retold stories of their father paying them for every copycat Ouija board they could find in toy magazines, such as those of the National Ouija Board Company of Washington, D.C. (LOC-PPDW.)

Washington Bowie IV (Junior) stands with his horse at Hermitage, a brick Colonial manor house built in 1750 by John Bowie Jr. The first occupant was John's grandson, Allen Bowie Jr., who was present in 1774 at the writing of the "Hungerford Resolves." During the Revolutionary War, Allen organized and paid his own company of troops. The house was the birthplace of Washington Bowie I, the "Merchant Prince of Georgetown," who lost his fortune in the War of 1812. A later owner, farmer J. P. Dodge, purchased 160 acres and the house. In 1914, Southwick Briggs and his wife purchased the house and were devoted to it. Briggs was the owner of the Briggs-Clarifier Company in Bethesda, which made oil filters for anything that needed one. He had many patents. Some business partners lived in Kensington. The property was sold to developers in 1951, and in the 1960s, the house was demolished with the construction of Fox Run. (MCHS.)

In the 1899 report to the state, this photograph—"Types of Bad Roads in Maryland—Turnpike Abandoned from Rough Surface, Montgomery County"—might be Rockville Pike. It shows the problem with a gravel road: washout. Along the Union Turnpike (Georgia Avenue), stones were partially furnished by farmers after plowing. They would gather them in piles along the road and be paid rates of 40¢ to 60¢ a perch. (Author.)

Road maintenance equipment owned by the county in 1899 included 15 road scrapers, 1 stone crusher, and a 3.5-ton horse roller. Over three-fourths of the wagons had tires more than 3.5 inches wide. Besides roadside perches, stone was taken from a quarry near Rock Creek—possibly on the Perry farm. The horse roller cost $300 (excluding horses). (Author.)

By 1899, the state had begun supplying expertise on road issues. This Maryland Geological Survey (1907) shows the towns of Wheaton and Plyer. Local government had always dealt with disputes over neighbors' lapsed maintenance but now took an expanded role. Roads, unlike railroads or canals, had not developed from public funds. The eastern portion of the county was well distributed with trap-rocks, granites, gneisses, and sandstone—a major factor in keeping roads maintained. Wheaton's tollgate keeper, Hezekiah Magruder, charged the users by the mile. Starting at 1¢ for a horse and rider or a horse and a vehicle—a 1/2¢ added if a pleasure carriage—the cost went up a penny for each added horse. It was 5¢ for all vehicles propelled by steam, electricity, or any motive power other than animal. Herded animals were charged 3¢ a "score," and broad-tread wagons (4 inches or over) received a 1/3 deduction off the total cost because of their wider wheels, which caused less road damage. Bicycles and tricycles paid a toll until exempted by law in 1900. People going to or from funerals were not charged, nor were those going to regular church or meetings on Sunday. (Author.)

Charles Webster and Jane Digings are pictured at their 50th wedding anniversary in 1918. Charles Webster was born in 1842 in South Carolina. During the Civil War, he crossed a river searching for his brother, who was supposedly watering the horses of Union troops bivouacked near their home. The troops burned the bridge—Charles couldn't swim, so he remained with the unit throughout the war. At war's end, an officer aboard a ship anchored at the pier in Washington, D.C., invited him to a dinner consisting of chicken and biscuits. While eating, the ship pulled out and went to South America; for three years, he mined bat guano, a natural manure. After returning to the United States, he was paid in $1 bills and began walking toward Maryland. He came upon the funeral of Ms. Digings and met the granddaughter of the deceased, Jane Digings, his future bride. (Sewell Horad family.)

Charles Webster built a house at Wheaton in the 1890s. Wheaton was merely an embryo of a community—scarcely populated and rural in every aspect. He owned about three acres of land but leased and farmed much of the surrounding acreage. With the help of his large family and hired hands, he grew, harvested, and sold produce to markets in Washington, D.C. (Sewell Horad family.)

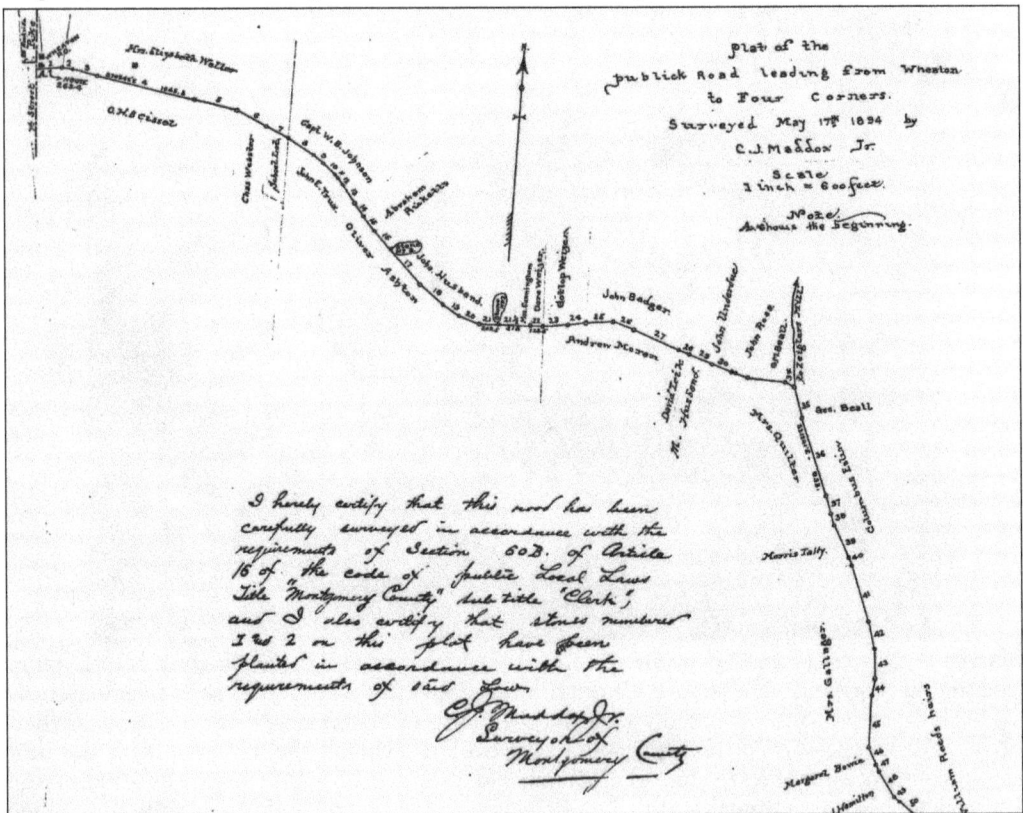

Charles Webster is shown as a property owner on a survey map done for the "Road from Wheaton to Four Corners" (University Boulevard). It is listed as a public road and not a toll road. Only owners would be listed on maps, not tenants or those leasing property. The Wheaton Post Office is now marked at the site of Mitchell's (by then G. O. B. Cissel's) Tavern. (MSALR.)

The Webster and Sewell family is shown around 1902 before or after a Sunday dinner, which was a traditional gathering of family and friends. Mr. Harris and his wife would travel from Washington, D.C., and as a professional photographer, he would bring along his camera. Pictured, from left to right, are (first row) Percy Webster, Florence Webster, Delsie Webster (Carter), Elsie Sewell (Horad), and Clarence Webster; (second row) Nan Webster Lewis, Charles Webster, Webster Sewell, Jane Webster, and Martha V. Webster Sewell; (third row) Oscar Webster, John Lewis, Mrs. Harris (photographer's wife), Edward B. Sewell, and Forest Webster. Missing are Edward, Charles, John, Ernest (who died at three years old), and Glendora. Jane Webster Sewell first lived in Barnesville, Maryland, in 1890 before moving to Wheaton. On Sundays the family would visit old friends like Mrs. Mary Brown driving in the family's Ford. The 30-mile drive would have taken a large part of the day with the drive being part of the fun. (Both Sewell Horad family.)

Thomas A. Johnson and his wife, Catherine A. Stewart Johnson, in 1868 farmed on the family property at Comus near Sugar Loaf Mountain and attended Boyds First Presbyterian Church. In the 1890s, they leased land at Bucklodge near one of the shipping centers that gave dairy farmers access to the Washington market along the Metropolitan Branch of the railroad. People, who prior to the railroad would never have met, attended meetings at the Methodist campground at Washington Grove, and social circles grew. Travel that had taken days took hours. Children moved away seeking employment in the city, and there were new professions. One Johnson son (Thomas) became an electrician and tragically ended his life at 27 when illness prevented him from practicing his trade. Two of their other sons would follow a more traditional path and move south to run a dairy operation. (Mary Hertel.)

One of Thomas and Catherine's sons, George Washington Johnson, married Alta Beatrice Walter on September 1, 1908, at St. John's Catholic Church in Forest Glen. They lived in Kensington after their wedding, and it is possible he was employed with the railroad. Alta was raised in Kensington but had been born in 1883 in Blocktown not far from Boyds. It is speculation that the rails brought them together. George went back to farming sometime between 1913 and 1915. They rented what was known as the "Old Perry Farm" in Wheaton, but still within walking distance to Kensington and Alta's family. They would have six children: George, Leonard (died when he was two), Walter, Mozell ("Gregory"), Paul, and Charles. Alta outlived her husband, and at her death at the age of 89 in 1973, she had 24 grandchildren and 29 great-grandchildren. (Mary Hertel.)

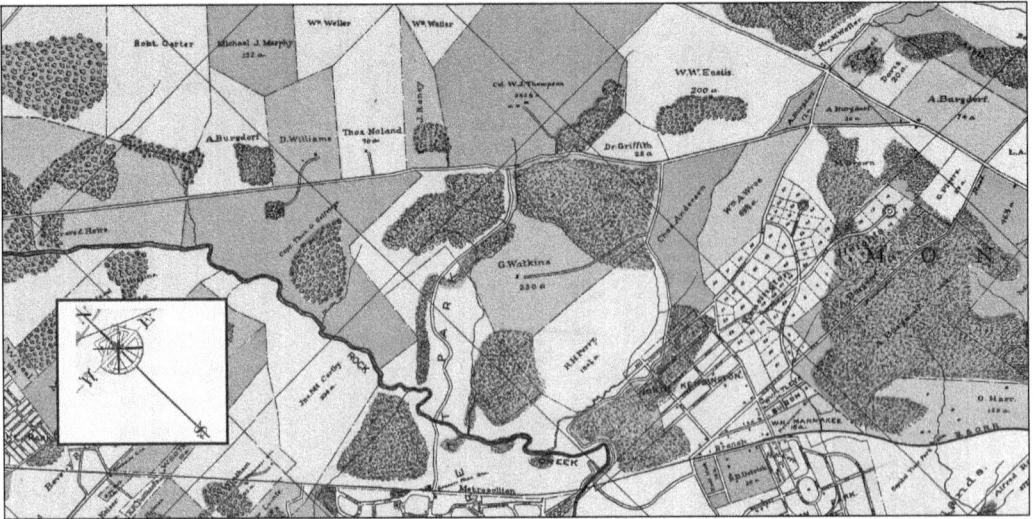

Land value rose rapidly from $25 an acre in 1882 to $350–500 an acre along the rail lines in 1892. This real estate map from 1890 was done for Metropolitan Branch of the Baltimore and Ohio Railroad Company. Early subdivisions would exist only in plat books for many years. In the lower right is the new town of Kensington, and farther north is the Perry farm. (LOC-GMDW.)

The Perry farm had been abandoned for a number of years, and the house needed work before the Johnsons could live there. By 1914, a swing set was in the front yard. The address was Veirs Mill Road with access by a lane connecting first to Newport Mill Road. The house was located at the site of Rock View Elementary School. (Mary Hertel.)

Four

COUNTRY PASTIMES AND RAISING FAMILIES

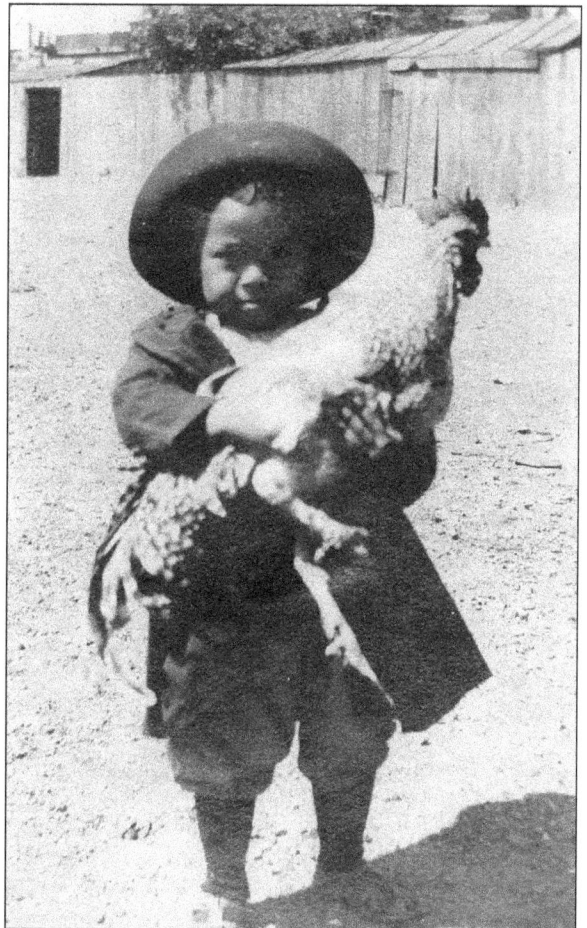

In 1910, Bernard Fulton Sewell had a pet chicken, not on his grandparent's farm in Wheaton but at his parent's house on Twenty-second and P Streets in Georgetown. It was a different city. He would in the years to come graduate from Howard University, receive a master's degree from Columbia University in New York, and work as a teacher and administrator in the D.C. Public Schools for 43 years. (Sewell Horad family.)

Charles Webster (far left) built a "play house" for his granddaughter Elsie Sewell Horad under the great oak tree in the front yard. The front porch was a gathering place for family and friends. Elsie remembered her life at Wheaton as a happy experience. (Sewell Horad family.)

Born in Wheeling, Virginia, in 1850, Jane Digings Webster never recognized West Virginia as a state and always said she was born in Virginia. Her marriage to Charles Webster led to the birth of 13 children—8 boys and 5 girls—the first generation of free blacks. Education of African Americans was against the law. However, her daughter Martha V. Webster, born in 1874, got through the third grade. (Sewell Horad family.)

Jane (middle left) and Charles Webster (middle right) are seen with visitors on the farm on Bladensburg Road (University Boulevard) sometime in the late 1920s. Visiting was one form of entertainment, the county fair another. Jane Webster would fry a barrel of chicken to take to the weeklong event, and Elsie Sewell Horad, her granddaughter, remembered that while the chicken cooked no one was allowed as much as a gizzard to taste. (Sewell Horad family.)

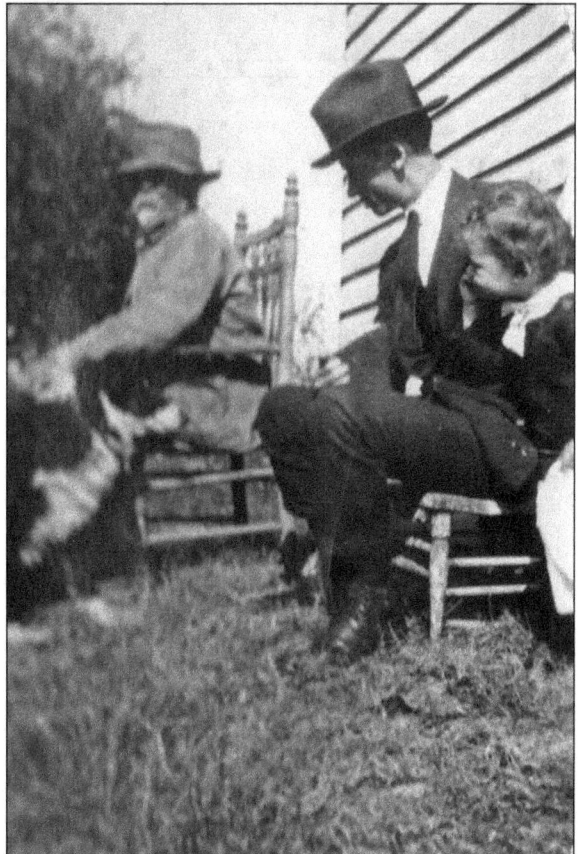

Three generations of family are pictured here: Charles Webster, Romeo W. Horad Sr., and Romeo W. Horad Jr. The favorite grandchild of Charles Webster, Elsie Sewell, married Romeo Horad Sr., a real estate broker in Washington, D.C. The family visited often, bringing their young sons Romeo and Sewell to their great-grandparents' farm. Charles Webster died in 1927 not long after this photograph was taken. (Sewell Horad family.)

Martha V. Webster (second from left) married Edward B. Sewell in 1897. They belonged to the Queen Esther Players, a theater group that mainly focused on biblical dramas. One time, Edward was supposed to stab himself but got a little carried away and had to be rushed to the hospital. The show was not stopped since it was the last scene. (Sewell Horad family.)

Webster Sewell (left) and Edward Benjamin Sewell (right) are shown on the Mall in Washington, D.C. As far back as the Sewells can trace, there were no slaves in the family. Before moving the family to Wheaton, the Sewells lived at 2442 P Street NW in Georgetown. The south side had three tiny houses, and they lived in the middle one. Farm animals grazed in the valley behind the house. (Sewell Horad family.)

Alta Walter sits on the front porch of the old farmhouse at the Perry farm. Walter (left) and Leonard (right), who was born on the farm, are the two children playing in the front yard. The photograph was taken in 1916 just before Leonard died. (Mary Hertel.)

The Perry farm doubled its workforce in 1919, when George's brother Oliver Granville Johnson and his wife, Ida Jane Kuster Johnson, and their growing family moved to the dairy farm. Although younger than his brother, Oliver had married first in 1892. Ida's brother Charles worked for the railroad. (Mary Hertel.)

Over half the farmers in Montgomery County within 3 miles of the railroad were in the diary business in the 1920s, and the Johnsons were among them. Above, Oliver Johnson waits for the cows and cleans the barn at the Old Perry farm around 1930. A dairy farm negated the need for heavy fertilizers for crops, but corn would have been grown for feed and perhaps as produce for the local market. The bulk of the land would be pasture. Many of the newcomers had moved to Kensington to enjoy the atmosphere of the farm life they had grown up with but absent the hard labor. A farm nearby helped set the scene. The people of both the town and the city were ready customers for the milk, and the rail line shipped excess products. (Both Mary Hertel.)

Mamie Lucille Johnson (far left) had been born in Buckeystown, Maryland, in 1910 and was nine years old at the time her parents moved the family to Wheaton. She is pictured on the farm with her sisters Lillian (far right) and Mary (front). They would attend the school in Kensington. She always told her children that behind the old farmhouse was a Native American grave. (Mary Hertel.)

In 1927, the daughters of Oliver and Ida Johnson were preparing for a wedding on the farm. All the sisters would take part. Pictured from left to right are (first row) Lillian, Lucille (the bride to be), and Ella; (second row) Mary and Myrtle. Mary worked for the telephone company in Kensington and later for the government. (Mary Hertel.)

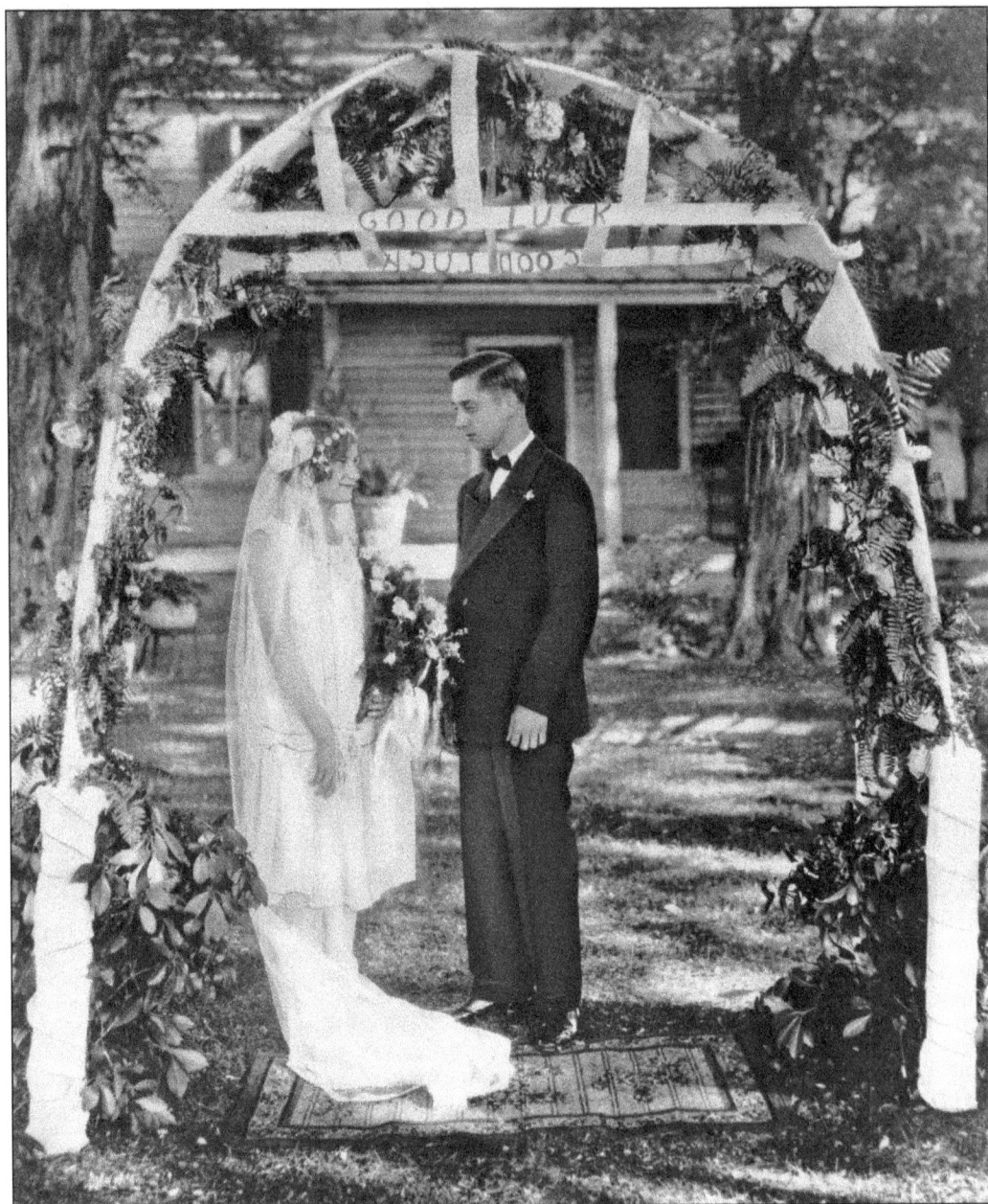

Just shy of her 17th birthday, Mamie Lucille Johnson married Martin Dewhite Wolfe in 1927. He was 21. Their five children would be raised within walking distance of the old farm and play in its fields just as their mother had. Ida Johnson, Mamie's mother, died in 1931. Oliver Johnson, Mamie's father, had stopped farming and moved to Lawrence Avenue in the early years of the Depression. The young couple lived with him when their daughter Mary Wolfe Hertel was born. They would get a home of their own a few lots away on Newport Mill Road. Both of these houses are still standing. In the early years to support his family, Martin Wolfe worked many jobs, and one time while returning home from the Piggly Wiggly in Kensington he was robbed. He became an employee for the WSSC in Prince George's County. His children were not allowed to ride in the company truck no matter how deep the snow. (Mary Hertel.)

Sewell Horad had a great-uncle who lived in Atlantic City, so every summer included a visit and a few weeks at the beach. Much of the remaining summer was on the farm in Wheaton. Sewell, here around 1924, remembers carefree country living with a garden to pick and chickens, ducks, guinea fowl, and geese. Mornings were the time to gather eggs and feed chickens. (Sewell Horad family.)

"Come to a fox hunt at the home of Mr. and Mrs. George Plyer, corner of Brookeville Turnpike and Plyers Mill Road'" was the invitation extended to many Wheatonites at the dawn of the 20th century. Times were listed in the local papers, and the Chevy Chase Hunt Club met there often at the start of a hunt. (LOC-PPDW, Theodor Horydczak Collection.)

Walter T. Magruder in the later years of his life owned and raced horses. He traveled all over the world following the races. His horses raced locally at nearby racetracks, and some were kept in shape during the winter months by being sent to tracks in the South. Walter died of tick fever in 1938 after being bitten by a tropical tick while in Cuba with the races. No serums existed at that time. Walter T. Magruder is holding the reins of his horse Cornbelt, being ridden by jockey E. Shropshire in New Orleans on March 5, 1922. The home he built in 1903 is now part of Wheaton Regional Park and occupied by the Park Naturalist. (Both Christopher M. Stubbs.)

American Legion Cissel-Saxon Post's horse show on May 25, 1929, at Kensington and Brookeville Roads (University Boulevard and Georgia Avenue) had fair weather and a large crowd. Cars parked in a circle to form the show ring on the land for the Lutheran College for Women (never built). The previous owner would have been pleased. The grandson and heir of W. W. Corcoran (Corcoran Gallery of Art), William ("Willie") Corcoran Eustis had studied law and was marked for diplomatic service but never pursued any career. At the age of 50, he volunteered and served in World War I. His true interests in life were horses and hunting. These fields had been training tracks for his racehorses. In 1878, it had been the Burdette farm, and around 1880, Col. George Rust from Virginia owned the property. (LOC-PPDW, Theodor Horydczak Collection.)

Capt. Joseph C. Cissel, Mrs. Andrew J. Cummings of Bethesda, Col. William Mitchell, and Capt. Henry C. Butler of the Maryland State Police were judges of the 65 entries from Maryland, Virginia, and D.C. Missing from the program were the same-day arrivals. The Cissell-Saxon Post was named in honor of Lt. Carroll Cissell, 115th Regiment, 29th Division, World War I, the son of G. O. B Cissell. (LOC-PPDW, Theodor Horydczak Collection.)

Bandit Flag, entered by C. W. Rust, was awarded the trophy as the best horse in the show. Prizes were awarded for the best-dressed man and the best-dressed woman—a season pass to the Laurel Racetrack. The ninth class (an added feature), women hunters had four runoffs to decide the event and turned out to be the most popular of the show. (LOC-PPDW, Theodor Horydczak Collection.)

The winner of the first class, Ponies Shown Under Saddle, was First Billy. The attendees hoped for an annual event. The following year, the Cissel-Saxon Post had other concerns, and a committee to aid the jobless urged every resident of the county to have painting, papering, and carpentering go to unemployed servicemen. (LOC-PPDW, Theodor Horydczak Collection.)

Edward B. Sewell was a baseball player and had all of the equipment—gloves, balls, bats, and a catcher's mask. He played on a league and with his grandchildren whenever possible. He worked for the Bell Telephone Company for 37 years, rising at 4:00 a.m. He would drive into the city and park at Eleventh and S Streets NW and walk many blocks to the telephone company. (Sewell Horad family.)

After the war, traveling tent circuses arrived. In Wheaton, the big top unfolded at Godfrey's Corner (Kensington-Wheaton Road and Veirs Mill Road). The Wheaton Lions Club and Wheaton Chamber of Commerce sponsored performances for fund-raising. In 1954, two benefit performances were held by the Mills Brothers Circus for the new Wheaton High School Athletic Fund in hopes of raising $5,000. Several appearances were made in the 1960s of the 73-year-old Bartok (formerly Hunt Brothers) Circus. Their tent went up at Wheaton Plaza to the delight of the children of the area. Not many traveling circuses remained by this time (four or five), and Doc Milton Bartok, who started with a medicine sideshow, still personally operated the circus. The animals—elephants and "chocolate browns" (circus term for bears)—were important, but he believed the audience came to see "flesh." (WKCC.)

Five

THE COMMUNICATION
AGE BEGINS

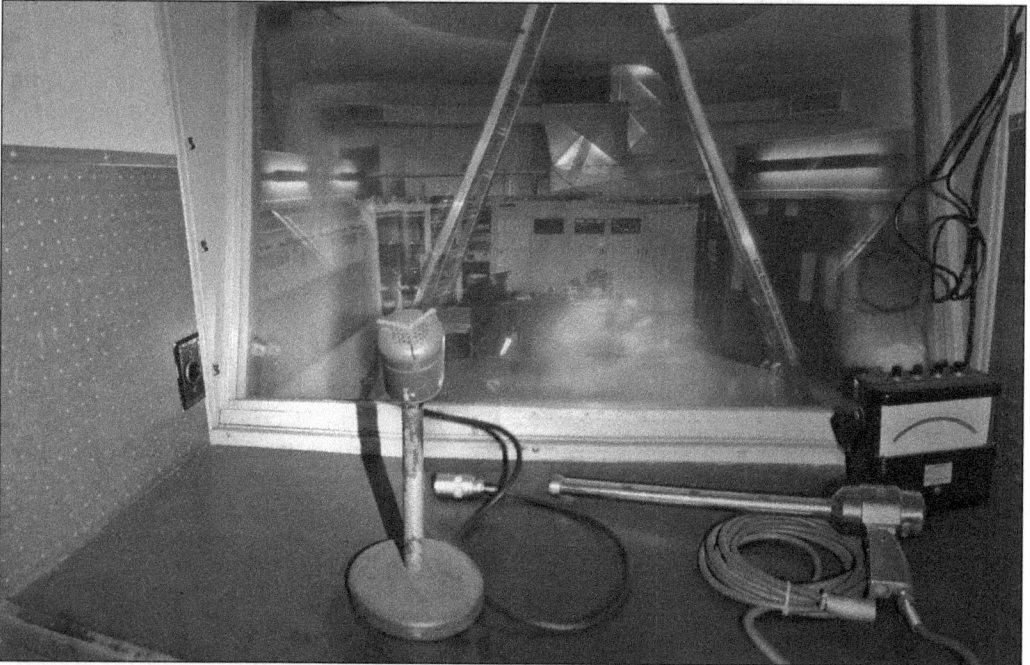

Wheaton became the birthplace of the first television transmissions from Jenkins Broadcasting and the home for the transmitters of WTOP, WGAY/WQMR, and WDON/WASH for the same reason—the highest sea level peaks in the Greater Washington area. All stations (except WTOP) had broadcasting studios in Wheaton. WTOP did install a booth in the mid-1960s for late-night classical music, but the broadcast was short-lived. (Author.)

The first U.S. television license, W3XK (1928), operated out of Charles Francis Jenkins home in Wheaton. He is inspecting the apparatus that will be used to make the first national broadcast of motion pictures by radio on July 2, 1928. In 1923, he transmitted moving silhouette images for witnesses, and it was June 13, 1925, that he publicly demonstrated synchronized transmission of pictures and sound. (LOC-PPDW.)

Jenkins in 1894 outlined a scheme for the electrical transmission of pictures and in 1913 suggested wireless moving-picture news. In December 1924, clear images of the signature of Herbert Hoover, then secretary of commerce, were sent 450 miles to Boston. In 1925, a mechanical scanning system (revolving disk with tiny lenses) was demonstrated. A year later, when Jenkins was collaborating with the navy, a mysterious radio "pen" flashed weather maps to sea. (LOC-PPDW.)

Jenkins erected two 100-foot steel transmitting towers for the earliest scheduled television service in the country outside his home/broadcasting studio (the house behind the tower). The short-wave station began transmitting across the eastern United States from Wheaton on a regular basis on July 2, 1928. The "Radiomovies" were broadcast five nights per week until 1932. (WKCC.)

Jenkins Radio Movie Broadcasting Station operated from 1929 to 1932, and the house (Georgia Avenue and Windham Lane) is a registered historic landmark. Charles Francis Jenkins (born in Dayton, Ohio) arrived in D.C. in 1890, and his first invention—the Phantascope, an early movie projector—was perfected at Bliss School of Electricity with Thomas Armat. Jenkins was also the founder of the Society of Motion Picture Television Engineers (SMPTE). (Author.)

Jenkins, adjusting the main transmitting panel, also broadcast and directed the earliest regularly scheduled television shows, consisting of teleplays enacted by staff and neighbors. Receiving the signal was a multi-tube radio set with a special picture-receiving attachment. By 1928, several thousand sets had sold. Costs varied between $85 and $135. The device consisted of an electric motor and prismatic rings. It managed to produce a cloudy 40-line image on a 6-inch square mirror. He also invented a radio conversion kit that sold for $7.50. Jenkins was a holder of over 400 patents—75 pertaining to mechanical television alone. In explaining his invention, he said, "It's easy. Don't you remember when we were little tykes, mother entertained us by putting a penny under a piece of paper, and by drawing straight lines across the paper, she made a picture of the Indian appear? Well, that's the very way we do it. The incoming radio signals turn the light up and down as it moves swiftly over the screen and you see the distant scene." (LOC-PPDW.)

The cut-away is the final design of the WJSV (WTOP) transmitter building done by local architect E. Burton Corning in 1939. He did work in the modern style, but his client (CBS) had definite ideas about the project. In 1928, William Paley purchased and named CBS (Columbia Broadcasting System). Besides broadcasting, Paley was on the board of directors at the Museum of Modern Art and was interested in the visual arts. He was concerned with CBS having a distinctive corporate look that extended to every aspect of the operation. Projecting a positive, confident, competent image of the corporation to federal regulators, commercial sponsors, company employees, competitors, and the general public was the goal. Design was used to communicate. The view along the front porch shows the art deco elements of the door. (Both Bonneville International.)

Shown here is construction of the wooden framework for the reinforced concrete walls of the WJSV (WTOP) transmitter building. It was said at the time that the structure of the circular building when it was completed was so strong that if it were turned over on its side, it could be rolled along the ground without coming apart. The work crew photograph was taken on December 18, 1939, and processed on archival linen paper. Everyone involved with the project felt he or she were making history and wanted the record to last the ages. Most (if not all) of the early WJSV photographs were the work of Theodor Horydczak, a Washington photographer who documented the architecture and social life of the Washington metropolitan area from 1920 to 1940. Unfortunately, the names of the work crew are unidentified. (Both Bonneville International.)

This view looks west toward the finished WJSV (WTOP) transmitting plant. Note the fields and wide-open spaces that existed in 1939 when building construction started. The short pole to the right of the "A" tower is the "gin pole" used to erect the 350-foot antenna towers. It was "planted" in the ground to be used for one end of an emergency "flat-top" antenna; the other end tied to the rear of the transmitter building. Transmitters could be switched to this emergency antenna in case of failure of the antenna phasor or if one or more of the main antenna towers fell down. In the field are sections of antenna towers lying on the ground before erection. (Both Bonneville International.)

In January 1940, the narrow road in front of the WJSV (WTOP) transmitter building was Old Bladensburg Road, since widened and renamed University Boulevard. Property had to be released to the county for the widening. Across the road is the farm of the Websters and the Sewells and in the lower left is their farmhouse. (Bonneville International.)

The "C" tower coupling house, called a "doghouse," sits next to "C" tower base. Note the chicken wire on the cement pad. This is special copper chicken wire. When the wire was sent out to be plated, the plater asked what kind of chickens were so special that they needed copper-plated wire. (Bonneville International.)

Being stationed in Wheaton in 1940 was to be in the middle of nowhere. Live-in facilities for the engineers at the transmission station were provided if needed, such as when trapped due to bad weather. This apartment had an enclosed kitchen, and the closet to the left contained a Murphy bed; restroom with shower is to the right. The original kitchen and bathroom are still in place. (Bonneville International.)

The curving streamlined design of the outside of the building is matched on the inside. Looking down the main stairway from outside the office door, the stark character of the international style boldly proclaimed the novelty of the new medium of radio. No attempt was made to disguise or camouflage the equipment required by the facilities. (Bonneville International.)

This WJSV (WTOP) technical crew installed the new Western Electric type 407a, 50,000-watt transmitter in 1940. Standing in front of the final amplifier stages, from left to right, are Clyde Hunt, chief engineer; Lewis Rice, transmitter technician; James Middlebrooks, CBS supervising engineer; two Western Electric engineers; William Kriz, transmitter supervisor; and Lynwood McDonald, transmitter technician. Hunt admitted to several weeks of four hours of sleep before opening day. (Bonneville International.)

Missing above (probably the photographer) is Granville Klink. He was responsible for construction of the WJSV (WTOP) transmitter facility and towers in Wheaton and was the radio engineer for Pres. Franklin D. Roosevelt. As chief engineer for WTOP-TV, Klink helped design and build the first microwave television system in 1953, used at the presidential inauguration. Klink here stands in 1966 with the Scully recording equipment in WTOP Radio Master Control. (Bonneville International.)

This is the installation of the Western Electric 50,000-watt Doherty transmitter in December 1939, with exciter cabinets at the left, driver and final amplifier cabinets in the center, and phasor cabinets at the right. The combination of new equipment and a new location allowed a gain of approximately 30 percent (about 200,000 new listeners) and an initial investment of $300,000. (Bonneville International.)

One of the WJSV (WTOP) transmitter men, Herman Groom, is seated at the control desk. There was a transmitter staff of seven men who covered the transmitter operation 24 hours a day, seven days a week. (Bonneville International, photograph by Theodor Horydczak.)

The call letters changed to WTOP in 1945. The transmitter building and antenna system are shown in the 1950s before the road was widened in front of the site and before the Dutch elm tree at the right of the building was removed by the county because of Dutch elm disease. WTOP is the only all-news radio station in the Washington, D.C., area. (Bonneville International.)

Historical designation was placed on the site in 1990. The reasons were the unique international style of the architecture (rare in the area) of the transmitter building and the fact that it is was the most powerful transmitter in Washington at the time of construction. Not everyone was pleased with the 4-3 vote granting historic protection. Councilwoman Rose Crenca (one of the three) called the building ugly among other comments. (Author.)

Two Wheaton landmarks at University Boulevard and Veirs Mill Road are Nick's Diner (owner Nick Markopoulos) and the self-supporting lattice transmission tower built by Don ("Everett") L. Dillard, president, general manager, and chief engineer of WDON and WASH-FM. The transmitters for both stations were in the single-floor brick building at the base of the tower along with the broadcast studio for WASH-FM. Dillard used WASH-FM to show off his Continental Equipment Company products to prospective customers building radio stations across the United States and Europe. The WDON-AM antenna connected with a wire that ran up the side of the WASH-FM tower. WASH-FM was later sold to MetroMedia for $10 million. (Author.)

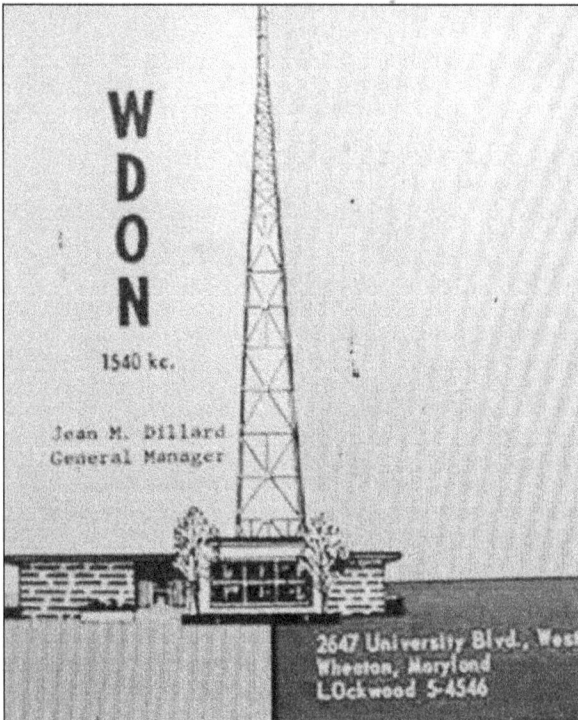

Everett Dillard, the original owner of WASH-FM, was an early pioneer in FM "networking" and stereo broadcasting. WASH-FM was licensed to Washington, D.C., in 1944. One system for the early stereo broadcasts was to broadcast one channel over WASH-FM and the other channel on WDON-AM 1540. During the 1940s, Dillard also headed the Washington-based Continental FM Network, a 52-station network. It was Dillard's and Edwin Howard Armstrong's creation to get some content for Armstrong's Alpine, New Jersey, station. Dillard's WASH-FM fed a 15-kilohertz phone line to New Jersey. Some of the content was WASH's evening classical program. After MetroMedia purchased WASH-FM in 1968, the studios and transmitter were moved to MetroMedia's Wisconsin Avenue headquarters and the WTTG-TV tower to D.C. (Both R. A. Campbell, RACampbell.com.)

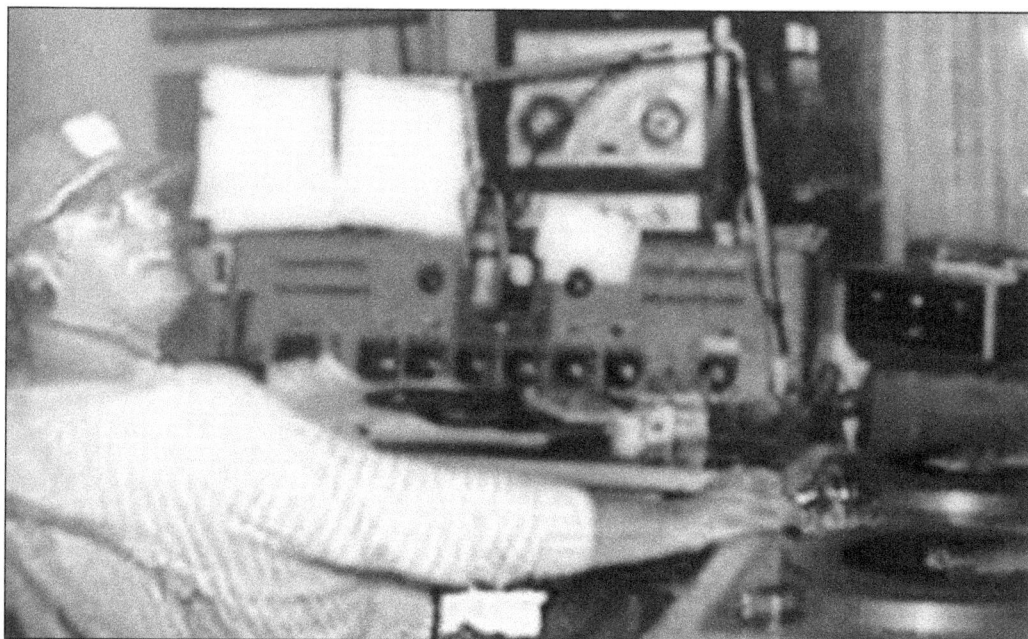

"Washington's Gold Rush" had a loyal audience regardless of an eclectic mix: rockabilly, rock 'n' roll, black and white doo-wop, rhythm and blues, oldies, and briefly "Disco D-O-N." The continuity was its ownership— Everett Dillard. Many radio talents would DJ from the studio in the Dunkin' Donuts strip mall. Don, the call letters' namesake and Dillard's son, is rumored to have greeted wanderers looking for a laundry confused by WASH/WDON on the door. Disc Jockey Hall of Famer Tom "Cat" Reeder's sign-off line—"I hope you live as long as you want, and never want as long as you live, bye-bye, darlin'"—can still be heard on WAMU's Blue Grass Country (bluegrasscountry.org). WDON converted to Spanish-format WMDO, "Radio Mundo" and now WACA "Radio America," owned and operated by Alejandro Carrasco. (Above R. A. Campbell, RACampbell.com; below author.)

Not even 10 years after opening on July 2, 1948, this aerial view of the Wheaton WTOP transmitter site shows all the new neighbors cropping up in the countryside. It isn't in the country anymore, but there is still no need for fencing. Looking toward Silver Spring in the upper left, the Washington Monument is visible in the skyline. Old Bladensburg Road (University Boulevard) runs in front of the transmitter, and across the road is the Sewells' orchards and farmhouse and the brick house the Horads built to live close to their family in 1938. The beginnings of the building boom that was about to engulf the area is evident with the new housing developments. Also visible on close inspection are the transmitter towers of WGAY and the Jenkins television towers. Georgia Avenue is toward the right. (Bonneville International.)

WGAY-FM was broadcast from the art deco building with glass bricks on Kemp Mill Road. Joseph Brechner, founder, was one of the pioneers of the commercial development of Wheaton. WHIP-FM's FCC permit on August 1947 was approved to transform 31 acres and a farmhouse, also on Kemp Mill Road, into Radio City. There is no evidence it ever made it to the airwaves, but a tower was built. (Bill Halverson.)

Mary Wolfe Hertel (center) is surrounded by her siblings, who are, from left to right, (first row) Diane, Martin, and Mickey Wolfe, in the front; (second row) Pansy Marie (Pat) and Charlotte Wolfe in 1950. Mary grew up playing on the Perry farm and walked to Kensington Elementary, then caught buses in Wheaton to go to Blair High School. As a teen, she and her cousin would walk to the WGAY station on Kemp Mill and sit and listen to their friend Don Owens play the "hillbilly" country music they liked. (Mary Hertel.)

Homemaker's Gift Shop and Florence, the Girl Disc Jockey, entertained listeners in the early years of WGAY. Regular broadcasts by students from Prince George's and Montgomery County schools, forum discussions with community leaders, and broadcasts by local ministers engendered much local pride in what people felt was "their station." Country music and local legend Don Owens got his start here when he was 14 after told by a friend "he couldn't." He was also a writer and publisher of country music and died in a car accident in 1963. WGAY's neighbors started arriving in 1954 with the development of Kemp Mill Estates. Jack Kay and Harold Greenberg of the Kay Construction Company built "prestige homes, at popular prices." Five home models were available to buyers—all models featured Hotpoint electric kitchens with the utilities in color. Prices ranged from $21,000 to $24,950. WQMR-AM, "Washington's Quality Music Radio," went on the air in 1960. Both sets of call letters were on the building. WQMR would move to the World Building in Silver Spring in 1965. (M-NCPPC.)

For those who have looked in vain for the old location of WQMR-AM and WGAY-FM at 11306 Kemp Mill Road, the address was converted to 1206 Arcola Avenue in 1967 when the road was widened. The station was located where the Kemp Mill Shopping Center and Kemp Mill Park were developed. Originally the area was to be entirely commercial, but nearby residents bitterly opposed the development; as a result, the developer removed 1.5 acres for the park to create a strong buffer between the two land uses. It was built and is maintained by the Maryland-National Capital Park and Planning Commission and dedicated in 1969 with the talents of the Northwood High School Band. (Both M-NCPPC.)

Six

THE COMMUNITY GROWS

On the one-lane Ara Drive, once part of the Bowie estate, the Linthicums and Denleys were the "egg men" supplying the new residents with deliveries from their farms. A grove of trees that had grown on the old Denley farm still remains, and the one-lane road has houses tucked between churches, apartments, and the Metro along the busy multi-lane Georgia Avenue. (Mary Hertel.)

H. C. Hickerson from Kensington moved his business in 1927, saying, "Wheaton is the place of the future," taking over the Cissell Store on the Union Pike (Georgia Avenue). The tollgate manned by Hezekiah Magruder was across the road. Hickerson's carried a variety of merchandise from loaves of bread to horse collars and sugar in barrels. Voting booths were in the back. (Photograph by Malcolm Walters, WKCC.)

In one of the stores Dr. Atchison of Washington built in 1928, McKeevers Ice Cream opened, adding to their operations in Kensington. They also delivered. This site would be the location of a series of gathering places serving food. During World War II, it was Paul's Place, then the Wheaton Inn, followed by Naylor's, and its last occupant was Anchor Inn. The building was recently demolished. (Photograph by Malcolm Walters, WKCC.)

74

George Flavius Linthicum is on the farm on Ara Drive with his poultry. People had multiple avenues of employment. Besides being an egg man for many years, he also owned and operated a maintenance and repair service for kitchen and laundry equipment. Poultry, like dairy, was a farming that required less expense and space to implement. He and his wife, Julia Madaline Walter Linthicum, lived on Ara Drive for many years and expanded the house. Julia Madaline (the sister of Alta Johnson) always owned at least one dog at all times. They would retire to Wheaton Woods in 1966 and kept up their lifelong interest in gardening. George died in 1980 and Julia in 2000. (Both Mary Hertel.)

In 1938, Elsie Sewell Horad and her husband, Romeo Horad Sr., built a house on Old Bladensburg Road (University Boulevard West) next door to the old farmhouse and commuted to their real estate brokerage in D.C. The house was built with a slate roof and copper gutters. It still stands and is owned by the Horad family. Webster Sewell, Elsie's brother, would teach at Little Rock University for tuition to attend Howard Medical School. Graduating in 1932, he was enlisted as a captain in World War I. Opening his office in part of the old farmhouse, he added an east wing for the waiting room. As the only black doctor in Montgomery County, he was denied membership in the county medical association because he could not be served at their dinner meetings at local country clubs. (Both Sewell Horad family.)

Bernard Fulton Sewell finished Howard University, received a master's degree from Columbia in New York, and worked as a teacher and administrator in the D.C. Public Schools for 43 years. Elsie Sewell Horad taught school in Washington for 37 years and would eventually run the family real estate brokerage. Dr. Webster Sewell graduated from Howard University Medical School and practiced medicine in Montgomery County. They would all agree that their mother, Martha V. Webster Sewell (seated with her husband, Edward B. Sewell), was the guiding influence in the household. She worked for Alexander Graham Bell, and a benefit was free phone service. When the bill arrived, she would write "this is correct," sign her name, and mail it back. (Both Sewell Horad family.)

In 1940, two-lane Georgia Avenue (right) and Kensington-Wheaton Road (University Boulevard, at left) were safe to drive at any speed. In 1922, Dr. Atchison of Washington built a gas station with an apartment above. The widening of "the Avenue of Progress" forced the ESSO to relocate across the road, and its catty-cornered neighbor, Hickerson's, was demolished. (WKCC.)

Home building was on the rise before the postwar boom but not on the commercial scale that would occur at that time. Earl Johnson was a builder, as were his sons, and in 1942, the Lithicums took a series of photographs while members of the Johnson family were building an addition to their home on Ara Drive. (Mary Hertel.)

Christmas of 1947 featured the Christmas Candle, a community tradition that would have only a few more seasons before storm damage forced its retirement. The ESSO station sits at the corner of Bladensburg Road (University Boulevard) and Georgia Avenue with the Wheaton Inn to the left. Across from the ESSO, the holly tree stands alone without Mitchell's Tavern, which had burned down in 1940. (William Scaggs family.)

In this sparse economic atmosphere, the Wheaton Chamber of Commerce formed in 1948. From left to right are (first row) John R. Pendleton Sr., board of directors; Thomas G. Oyster, president; and John E. Buffin, vice president; (second row) J. Milton Smith, secretary; and Robert Welch; (third row) John M. Smith, board of directors; Louis Rock; Robert Pendleton, treasurer; and John Pendleton Jr. Missing are E. S. Price and Lloyd Goebel. (WKCC.)

Commercial development was also at Veirs Mill Road and the Kensington-Wheaton Road (University Boulevard). In 1940, A. E. Godfrey built an Amoco station on the northeast corner, which became known as Godfrey's Corner. It is one place the traveling circuses would pitch their tents. His son-in-law "Mac" Horsman would later run the station. On the southwest corner, Goebel's Florists had a residence and greenhouses. They grew a variety of hothouse flowers for cutting and, like McKeevers Ice Cream Parlor, delivered to Kensington, Silver Spring, and Wheaton. Whenever the occasion demanded, all one needed to do was call Mrs. Goebel and tell her what was wanted, and she would send a beautiful arrangement. In an earlier time, a one-room frame school was located there. Gas stations stood on the other two corners. (MCHS.)

In 1948, Romeo W. Horad and a group of concerned black citizens conducted a survey of black county schools, finding them deplorable and unsafe and labeling them "dumps." Horad, an NAACP leader, led a small delegation to the county council to protest discrimination, saying he was not asking for the end of segregation, only that black children have the same chance at education as white children. The result was that the county purchased land for two new schools but foresaw no change in the "separate but equal" philosophy upheld by the U.S. Supreme Court in 1896 and had no plans to construct more than one high school for black students. George Washington Carver High School and Junior College and Rock Terrace Colored Elementary School opened for students in September 1951. After the decision of *Brown v. Board of Education* in 1954, the county proceeded slowly toward eventual integration; it was not until the 1960–1961 school year that 89 years of separate and unequal public education for Montgomery County's black student population ceased. (Sewell Horad family.)

Structures of all types were in demand at the end of World War II, and churches managed services in any location they could find. Hughes Methodist Church found Plyer's farmhouse inadequate for services and acquired a surplus army barracks donated by the Beltsville Methodist Church. They would later give the barracks to the First Baptist Church of Wheaton. (Hughes Methodist Church.)

While St. Catherine Labouré built their church, mass was celebrated by Fr. Stephen E. Byren and his congregation in the Viers Mill Theater at the corner of Randolph and Veirs Mill Roads. Sidney Lust, owner of the theater, allowed churches to use his cinema for Sunday worship services. Mass in the summer of 1950 meant sitting in comfortable seats but kneeling on the sloping floor. (St. Catherine Labouré.)

Sunday school classes for Hughes Methodist were at Oakland Terrace Elementary. In 1952, the first phase of building began, and Plyer's old farmhouse was torn down, never used for Sunday school occupancy because it was declared unsafe by the county building inspector. It was particularly lacking in fire exits. The first service was held on September 13, 1953, only five years after the first lawn tent meeting. (Hughes Methodist Church.)

St. Catherine Labouré's first mass was on All Souls Day in 1951. The chapel sits on a hill on the east side of Veirs Mill Road with the school behind and by 1955 had 1,000 pupils in six grades. The chapel is now used as a gym for the school. The open fields where foxhunters had run their hounds and horses were gone. (M-NCPPC.)

In 1947, the Lucy S. Owens family was lucky to move into their permanent home, the Old Brown House that had belonged to her aunt and uncle, Lucy (Leabeater) Speiden and Edgar Speiden I. The following year, it would be the first meeting place of the First Baptist Church of Wheaton. The family continued to live in the house for a year, and the home of their neighbors, the Veazeys, also began to be used for church purposes. (FBCW.)

The church grew, and the first chapel nears completion in February 1955. First Baptist was still using the army barracks from Hughes Methodist. The grounds are being prepared. The maple tree died in spite of efforts to save it. The Old Brown House was used for several more years. (FBCW, photograph Rev. B. Ross Morrison.)

In 1954, Viers Mill Village and Sydney Lust's Viers Mill Theater at Viers Mill Village Shopping Center (lower left) are getting new neighbors—Wheaton Woods and Connecticut Avenue Park. Besides being a temporary church, Viers Mill Theater had intermissions with local live acts, and the marquee's face would change from happy to sad. For a while, it was the only movie house from Rockville to Silver Spring and the place to be for children on a Saturday afternoon. As newer theaters were built, it lost business and was converted to X-rated films. It eventually became Rodman's Drugstore. The marquee was kept and displayed store specials until it caught fire. The last remaining part of the theater is the projection booth, which became the manager's office. Part of the forested area would become Matthew Henson State Park, a 2-mile-long stream valley greenway along Turkey Branch. The park connects Rock Creek Stream Valley Park Greenway with the Matthew Henson Greenway. (M-NCPPC.)

Viers Mill Village was built in 1948 as the second mass suburban development in the county. Twinbrook in Rockville was the first. "The houses appeared to be built over night" is the one point on which everyone seemed to agree. Brooklyn-based Harris Construction Company secured a contract to build 1,000 identical, 27-by-24-foot white-frame houses on a 330-acre tract of what had been the Selfridge dairy farm. (MCHS.)

Large areas of land in Wheaton were owned by developers (some since the 1890s), and sewer and waterlines were already installed. Development followed the work of the WSSC. City water arrived, and it was mandatory to fill wells. At the Sewells' farmhouse, another house was too far from the road to economically run the lines. Martha V. Sewell had the fire department burn the house down. (Sewell Horad family.)

The Wheaton Woods area, being developed in 1954, shows the construction method favored by builders: completely clearing the land. Concentrating on how fast they could put up homes, they preserved little as mass-production housing went up, in some cases at a pace of 10 houses a day. Factory methods produced the cost savings that kept the selling prices low and allowed thousands of families to own homes. (M-NCPPC.)

The *Evening Star*'s "Big Bertha" telephoto camera captured the symbolic view of the area's postwar development: many, many identical small houses. The camera and photographer were on the Wheaton water tower 150 feet from the ground on September 11, 1954. Pictured is a development in the Glenmont area. (Photograph by Francis Routt for the *Evening Star*, WKCC.)

Not all the house building followed the factory building methods. In 1958, Rock Creek Woods, designed by Charles Goodman, was constructed on part of what had once been the Perry farm. Goodman made every effort to preserve the indigenous trees and blend the houses into the existing topography. The homes full of innovative ideas were built between 1958 and 1961 by Herschel and Marvin Blumberg (Bancroft Construction Company). The 76 homes had only four models, but careful site placement created the appearance of many more. The original road to the houses followed the circuitous route that had led to the farmhouse, starting from Newport Mill Road, meandering through side streets, and allowing entrance via a narrow gravel road. Things would be made easier in 1964 when Connecticut Avenue was extended. The homes are on the National Register of Historic Places. (Author.)

Also designed by Charles Goodman are the 58 homes on 15 acres of Hammond Wood, tucked inside the larger Rock Creek Palisades neighborhood. These were built from 1949 to 1951, with "window walls" made of glass to take advantage of the wooded setting and make optimum use of natural light. They are also on the National Register of Historic Places as the Hammond Wood Historic District. (Author.)

Marketed as the "Home With All the Answers" by Standard Properties, the eight acres of development at Rock Creek Palisades replaced the farm the Johnsons had rented. The builder advertised they were the result of 18 months of research plus the construction of two experimental houses (1953–1954). Features included easy expansion and being closer to D.C. than the other subdivisions. Oddly, all the kitchens were built without drawers. (Author.)

Looking down Veirs Mill Road (in October 1954) west of University Boulevard, the results of the rapid pace of development are displayed. By this time, development closer to the Wheaton business district was intensive. Already in place was Hammond Hill, built in 1949 by Paul Bruman and Paul Hammond, partners in Hammond Homes, Inc., in collaboration with Montgomery County architect Charles M. Goodman. They constructed 20 small houses to sell at $10,500 each. In the seller's market of early 1950, all 20 were sold within a week of opening the model home for inspection. On the left are College View, Hammond Hills shielded by trees, and Connecticut Gardens. On the right are Monterrey Village, Wheaton Claridge Park, and the St. Catherine Labouré chapel and school building. Veirs Mill Road is still two lanes, and the spelling at the road signs is Viers Mill Road, a debate that continues with different branches of the Veirs/Viers families to the present day. (M-NCPPC.)

Seven

WHEATON COMMUNITY OF TOMORROW

The widening of Georgia Avenue helped create "The Community of Tomorrow." The surge of housing after World War II had produced the area's biggest woe—roads choking with traffic. The two-lane roads that intersected at Wheaton would turn into major highways. Getting people to and from their employment in Washington was the focus. Georgia Avenue as a six-lane solution had its ribbon-cutting in 1952. (WKCC.)

As the first building in Wheaton to have a water connection, Stubb's Grocery (Elbe's Beer and Wine) had its front entrance on the Kensington-Wheaton Road (University Boulevard). The building is sometimes described as the first office building—the top floor was the office of surveyor Thomas G. Oyster, and the bottom level was a beauty parlor. Howard's Beauty Salon would become Wheaton Beauty Salon. (Author.)

After losing his lease on his store in Silver Spring, William Bobrow bought Stubb's Grocery in 1951. He reopened in Wheaton the day after leaving Silver Spring as Elbe's Grocery, stocking fresh produce and meats. However, the arrival of supermarkets changed their market focus to beer and wines. This was a true mom-and-pop store; the Bobrows raised their children while running the business. (Bobrow family.)

Finished in 90 days, the million-dollar co-op opened before Christmas 1954. An acre of one-stop shopping and four acres of free parking included a 24-hour pharmacy, gas station, and a Food-O-Mat at the rear of the general store. Packaged products were fed via a monorail system slipping into place after a customer made a purchase. Quality Clothes Shop opened with door prizes being drawn by chamber president Victor Leisner. (WKCC.)

New businesses opened at a rapid pace at the Wheaton Crossroads. Montgomery County councilman Robert T. Snure and president of the chamber Victor A. Leisner attended the Wah Que Restaurant blessing at 11504 Old Bladensburg Road (University Boulevard) in 1955. The owners, the Gets, asked Reverend Wong, pastor of the Chinese congregation at St. Mary's Catholic Church, to perform the service. (WKCC.)

Although many believe all the farmland in Wheaton was suburban sprawl by 1950, this view looking south toward Silver Spring in 1953 shows the land east of Georgia Avenue still largely undeveloped. Along Old Bladensburg Road (University Boulevard), the transmission towers of WTOP are visible still with minimal fencing, and the Sewells' and Horads' homes across the road have a few neighbors. Wheaton Triangle's Central Business District, now zoned for commercial development, would have residential houses remain for several more years. The big issue was parking, and owners feared their property would be taken for the greater good. Grandview Avenue is cut through to join Veirs Mill Road, but members of M-NCPPC were concerned that traffic lights along Georgia Avenue for left-hand turns would hinder commuter traffic. Extensive construction caused problems for existing businesses and residences. Heavy rains caused the collapse of the addition being built onto Glenmont Elementary School, and flooding was the bane of Naylor's Seafood. Rats being displaced from their fields were also a headache for the county. (Walter Petzold.)

In the fall of 1954, M-NCPPC announced its opposition to the rezoning of the 79-acre Heitmuller Tract at Veirs Mill Road and Georgia Avenue, believing a department store could not make it in the area. Silver Spring and Bethesda intercepted all the business lying to the south of Wheaton. The chamber accused the commission of overstepping its boundary, trying to regulate competition, and promoting business monopolies. (M-NCPPC.)

Simon ("Si") Sherman was a local man living in Wheaton. He had attended Woodrow Wilson High School and National University and served in World War II and Korea. In 1947, he started Simon Construction Company. The local press reported, "He dreams dreams and then sets out to accomplish them . . . wishing to keep in the county all the proceeds from his development." His biggest dream was a mammoth shopping area—Wheaton Plaza. (WKCC.)

In December 1954, the Heitmuller Center (Wheaton Plaza/Westfield Wheaton) was rezoned. Si Sherman was deluged with calls, letters, and telegrams from as far west as Chicago for tenants. According to Sherman, "No expense will be spared to make this one of the finest shopping centers in the United States." The 4,000-car parking lot was one of the features influencing the county council in its rezoning decision. (WKCC.)

In March 1958, Woodward and Lothrop announced plans to build a $3-million, air-conditioned department store and had negotiated a long-term lease in the Wheaton Regional Shopping Center. The center would include 55 other stores and was expected to be ready for occupancy by the fall of 1959. A Giant Food supermarket, a Hot Shoppe restaurant, and a gasoline service station were already open. (WKCC.)

Wheaton Plaza was the fifth largest mall in the country. The open-air shopping center became universally known as the "Plaza," anchored by Woodward and Lothrop ("Woodies") on the east and Montgomery Ward on the west, with one level of shopping and a truck tunnel running under the plaza for the loading docks. This allowed virtually every store to have entrances both interior to the mall and exterior to the parking lot. Many of the area teenagers got their first jobs at the Plaza. The Orange Bowl, the Arcade, Hot Shoppes, Farrells, and Spencers Gifts are well remembered. Farrells was the place for birthday parties to delight a child or embarrass a friend with Green River sodas, ice cream volcanoes, and happy face sundaes. The delight or embarrassment was when a very exuberant staff marched out with drums and cymbals to sing "Happy Birthday" to the guest of honor. A special dessert made with 30 scoops of ice cream would also cause a mass demonstration as it made its way to its final destination. (M-NCPPC.)

By 1965, the Anchor Inn was closer to the corner thanks to road widening, and the Scaggs family made "the best cream of crab soup anywhere." Countless family and business celebrations occurred there over the years. The restaurant closed in 2004 after being sold to Greenhill Capital Corporation. The orange anchor illuminated the corner of Georgia Avenue and University Boulevard until the summer of 2008. (William Scaggs family.)

Looking due north over the Wheaton Triangle, the widened Veirs Mill Road and Georgia Avenue converge at the Co-op in the lower right. By 1964, they had a lot of retail company. Left turn lanes needed expanding to avoid long backups along Georgia Avenue as shoppers waited to turn into Wheaton Plaza (Westfield Wheaton); the area's traffic woes were still a deep concern. (WKCC.)

Janet Etheridge, Miss Wheaton in 1964, is pictured with the first Wheaton community entrance sign, erected as a project of the Wheaton Chamber of Commerce in conjunction with the many area service clubs. It was situated on land loaned by the Town and Country Day School on Veirs Mill Road. There was at least one other. A similar design was used for entrance signs in Silver Spring. (WKCC.)

The B. F. Goodrich store sold appliances and tires on the corner of University Boulevard. Opening in 1952, it was owned and operated by Ralph E. Graeves, who ran the business until his death in 1990. Good Time Old Fashioned Service is now there. The first Wheaton Library opened next door, and another neighbor was the *Wheaton News*, a local newspaper, run by Be Be Bailey. (Wheaton Regional Library.)

The chamber installed the Christmas lights for many years, and all the area merchants contributed to cover costs. From left to right are Ralph Graeves, of the retail merchants divisions; Harold Rowland, chamber president; and Charles Boynton, executive director, in December 1966. Ralph Graeves would also be a chamber president and served as director of the Wheaton Rescue Squad. Graeves received many awards for community service over the years, the last being the "Good Guy" award in 1989 from the Potomac Rotary Club. Chuck Boynton served as president and was the executive director many years in the first four decades of the organization. He also ran his own business—Wheaton Typewriter. Boynton spent much time preserving information about the area in scrapbooks for future researchers. However, the era of easy development was over by 1966. Increasing the size of the business district met strong opposition from area residents who felt that marginal businesses were already not paying their way and people were not willing to give up their new homes for endless road construction. (WKCC.)

The Washington Music Center known as "Chuck Levin's" moved from downtown Washington in 1968. The family-owned and operated company founded by Marge and Chuck Levin is now run by their sons. On October 26, 2003, hundreds of musicians, local citizens, government officials, and the U.S. Navy Commodores jazz band turned out to pay tribute to "a man who brought music to the world." The day is now officially "Chuck Levin Day" by the county. The Levin-Greenberg Building on the corner of Veirs Mill Road and Reedie Drive has a marker reading, "October 26, 2005, 'Chuck Levin Day' . . . featuring the Levin-Greenberg Sextet." Looking above the marker, one can see six relief panels created by the artist Phillip Ratner and gifted by the Leonard A. and Linda K. Greenberg Charitable Foundation in loving memory of Chuck Levin. (Both author.)

Eight

BUILDING COMMUNITY

Ted Englehardt designed the Glenmont Fire Station, at the corner of Glenmont-Colesville Road (Randolph Road) and Georgia Avenue, to hide the fact that the building is significantly larger on the inside than it appears. He accomplished this by using the combination of doghouse dormers in the front and a large shed dormer in the rear of the building, allowing for a large second-floor area. This gives the building a "residential" appearance while providing adequate space for the fire company. (David J. Kaplan.)

In 1951, the Kensington Volunteer Fire Department announced plans to build a new fire station that doubled as a community center. Badly needed, it was the second public service building in the area coming to the aid of the nearby Glenmont Elementary School. Local architect Ted Englehardt created a timeless Colonial style with a distinctive clock tower and an identifying landmark for the expanding neighborhood. He went on to design many buildings at the University of Maryland and several buildings at the National Institute of Health. Over 1,000 people attended the dedication on October 3, 1953, of what has turned out to be one of the largest celebrations for any new public service building in the county's history. It is threatened with destruction with the expansion of Randolph Road. (Both David J. Kaplan.)

The Wheaton and Kensington Chamber of Commerce has been involved in several beautification projects for the area, including the planting of trees in the medians. Some of these trees have survived. Walter Petzold is on the far left along with a representative of the Women's Club of Wheaton and several other volunteers at a median planting in the late 1960s. (WKCC.)

Displaying flags on national days of observance was a joint project. Funds were raised by the chamber of commerce to pay for the 120 nylon flags, and the Wheaton Volunteer Rescue Squad was responsible for putting up, taking down, and storing the flags. From left to right are chamber president Pat Tyser, chamber executive director Chuck Boynton, and Capt. Paul Friedlander of the Wheaton Volunteer Rescue Squad. (WKCC.)

The Wheaton Volunteer Rescue Squad was formed in 1955 and has served the community of Wheaton and surrounding areas of the county for over 50 years. They depend solely upon donations from the community (wvrs.org) and fund-raisers for financial support. The fleet of state-of-the-art emergency apparatus provides service 24 hours a day, 7 days a week, 365 days a year at no charge to those served. (WKCC.)

The Wheaton Volunteer Rescue Squad is involved in many community outreach programs and area health fairs. Angels for Children is a community effort involving the delivery of holiday presents to a selected group of children in the Wheaton area on Christmas Eve with a variety of elves, Mr. and Mrs. Claus, and, to the delight of the children, real rescue equipment! (Author.)

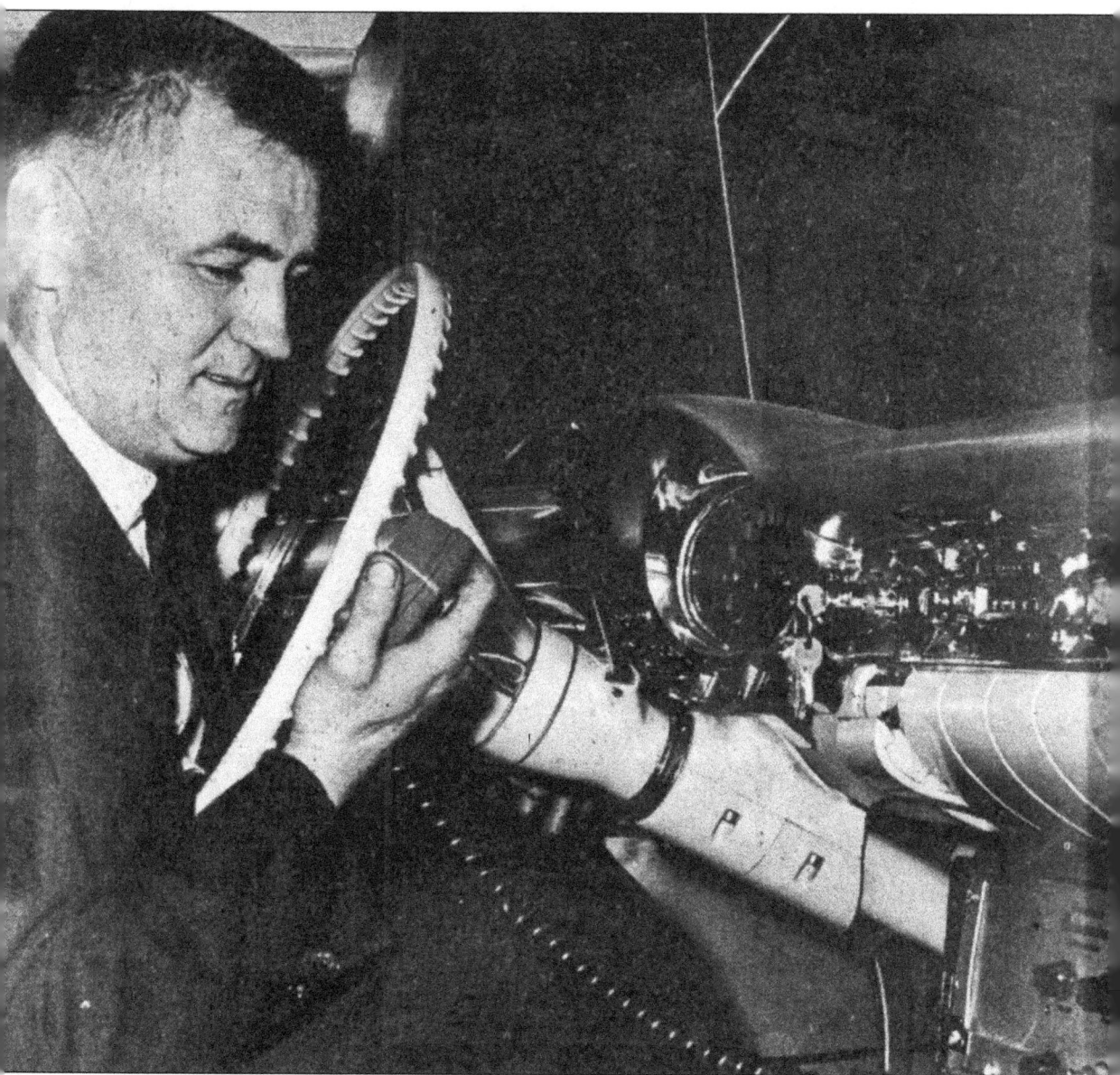

REACT—Radio Emergency Associated Citizens Teams—went on the air December 11, 1964, in a studio at the Howard Johnson's Motor Lodge. The local group of 230 volunteers started operations across the street in Uncle George's Ham Shack (Nick's Diner), which donated all the original equipment. They were glad to move into larger quarters. The group's purpose was to further public welfare through the application of two-way CB radio communications, to aid normal communications media in times of local or regional emergency disaster, and to promote the general understanding among non-radio users as to the potential of the citizen's band radio service. The two antennas located on top of the eight-story building could not have been bettered positioned, since the intersection of Veirs Mill Road and University Boulevard is 600 feet above sea level. Attaching the antennas to the building gave a height of 1,000 feet (almost twice as high as the Washington Monument). At one time, over 700 similar groups operated in the United States and were tied to the HELP—Highway Emergency Locating Plan. (WKCC.)

Wheaton Junior-Senior High School opened in 1954. It was the first school in the county built with federal money under Public Law 815, which provided aid to federally impacted areas. Opening with 1,400 students (7th to 11th grades), the school would add another 500 the next year. The driver training program was assured when Tom Amatucci of Tom's Chevrolet of Wheaton agreed to provide at least one car. (M-NCPPC.)

This is a Wheaton Boys Club sponsored football game in the 1960s. The organization is still active in its mission to promote juvenile decency through participation in youth sports programs, serving the children of Aspen Hill, Olney, Kensington, Silver Spring, Rockville, and Wheaton. The membership of 2,600 children is composed of a racially and ethnically diverse population that relies on volunteers to lead children in achieving their goals. (WKCC.)

Cpl. Fred Helton (center) is shown receiving the "1969 Policeman of the Year" award, presented by the Kiwanis Club of Wheaton, in the presence of his coworker Rocky (foreground) for apprehensions too numerous to list. Jack Ralph (left), president of the Kiwanis Club, and president-elect Chuck Boynton presented the award. (WKCC.)

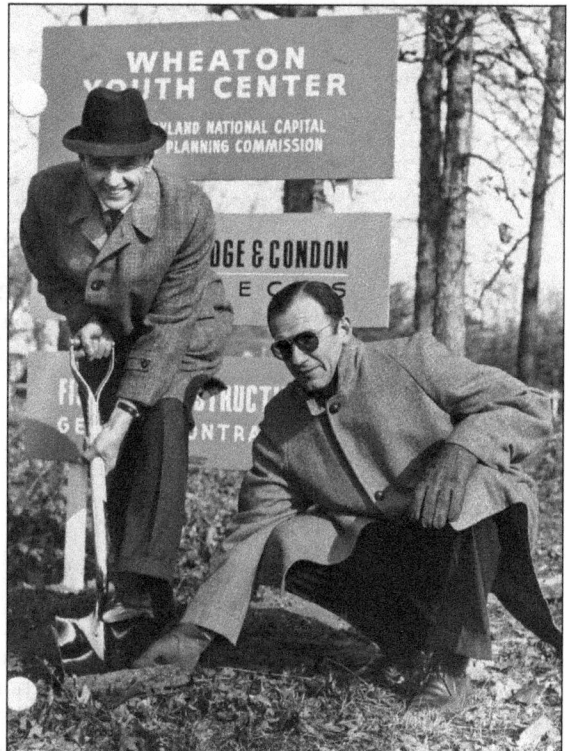

In 1963, ground was broken for the Wheaton Youth Center to provide leisure time activities for children. It now has activities for all age groups with fees for use of the facilities. A yearly pass is available. Various rock groups performed there, and it is rumored Led Zeppelin played on January 20, 1969, for the princely sum of $300. (M-NCPPPC.)

Schools filled fast, and double shifts were seriously considered. In 1956, Northwood Junior-Senior High was one of four brand-new schools ready after summer vacation. A two-story, H-shaped structure on a rolling tract on Old Bladensburg Road (University Boulevard) at Kemp Mill Road (Arcola Avenue) was an investment of $2 million. Closed in 1985 because of a declining population, it was used while other high schools were renovated. It reopened in 2004. (M-NCPPC.)

An order of condemnation at Georgia and Arcola Avenues by the county council was approved in 1959, and by 1962, the Wheaton Library had a new home. People complained of the odd check-out system determined by the week not the day, the nuisance of no renewals, the shortage of books on the shelves, and the battle to get in and out of the parking lot. (Wheaton Regional Library.)

Hanging in the two-story atrium of the Wheaton Regional Library is the metal and glass sculpture *Exploring Machine* by artist Julio Teich. It is a stabile, stationary sculpture that conveys a sense of movement in its sweeping curves. The artist was born in Buenos Aires in 1934 and began his artistic career working in paper collage. He died in 2000. He created Festival Bridge, which spans Wilson Boulevard (completed in 1996) at the Ballston Metro in Arlington. Julio's name was originally Teichberg, but he used Teich for his art. He was a descendant of Ralph Teichberg, whose name appears on the "Teichs on the Wall" (the American Immigrant Wall of Honor on Ellis Island, New York). The selection of the piece was made in 1986 from three-dimensional models submitted by three semi-finalists out of 152 artists. Each artist was paid $500 for producing his or her model. The final commission of $20,000 included installation of the 350-pound sculpture locked into the main structural beams of the building. The dedication was in the spring of 1988. (Author.)

Maryland-National Capital Park and Planning Commission first dealt with zoning to preserve appearance and property values. In 1928, their attention went to parks and they employed noted landscape architect Roland W. Rogers to plan a park system for the metropolitan district. He recommended that the whole system of stream valleys could be developed for parks "by using in almost every case only such land as was unfit for building purposes." The parks would encourage suburban development because "in most cases the park areas will be bounded by border roads which will afford the adjoining property owners park boulevard frontage and in theory materially increase the value of their land for real estate purposes." The first stream valley park was Sligo Creek Parkway, with almost all the land necessary donated by E. Brooke Lee and other adjoining property owners. (M-NCPPC.)

The largest recreational development in the metropolitan area, Wheaton Regional Park was a verdant island amid the housing developments. A stream was dammed to create Pine Lake and stocked with fish. Compared to New York's Central Park, it owed its existence to planners who foresaw the need of recreation facilities. The M-NCPPC staff had managed to convince landowners to wait as funds became available to purchase their property. County citizens fully supported the expanding park. Scouts of Troop 768 in 1968 work on scraping and painting close to 200 picnic tables to keep the park in shape. One-fourth of the area would be devoted to intensive "play use" and the rest left in its natural state. (Both M-NCPPC.)

The Nature Center at Wheaton Regional, pictured in 1961, featured natural history exhibits and demonstrations, a trailside museum, a 3/4-mile self-guiding nature trail, aquatic study pond, weather station, and live animal displays. Trail walks with a staff naturalist were available for organized groups, and many schools made the park the destination of field trips. (Photograph by Leet-Melbrook, Inc., M-NCPPC.)

On Veterans Day, November 11, 1965, the War Memorial was dedicated by Wheaton Post 268 and the community. The invocation was given by Rabbi Joseph M. Brandriss, Congregation Har Tzeon, Wheaton; the dedication of prayer by Rev. Robert L. Marston, pastor, Christ Congregational Church. The firing squad was the Maryland National Guard. "Taps" was played by the U.S. Air Force, and the benediction was given by Rt. Rev. Msgr. W. Joyce Russell, St. Catherine Labouré Church. (Photograph by Leet-Melbrook, Inc., M-NCPPC.)

Old MacDonald's Farm was a school field trip outing for many enrolled in Montgomery County's schools and one of the most vivid memories for many people who grew up in Wheaton. It was advertised as "a Maryland farm in miniature, with barn and silo, windmill, smokehouse and the young of our domestic animals grazing in the barnyard. An education for the youngsters and a touch of nostalgia for the oldsters." The farm had a variety of farm animals, including mules, ducks, pigs, chickens, and sheep. It was located in the playground area of the park. It seems rather fitting that it was on the land that had once been owned and farmed by the Magruders and the Stubbs families. (Both M-NCPPC.)

The park had scheduled events and activities in all seasons of the year. In winter, maple sap was boiled down at the log cabin at the Nature Center. Hot syrup was tossed in the snow to create an instant treat, if the weather cooperated. The warmer weather included the Summer Twilight Concerts. The first was on June 25, 1964, at the picnic grounds, and listeners brought their own chairs. Usually marching bands and sometimes jazz musicians played. The concerts, held in July and August, were free. The park still sponsors summer concerts in Brookside Gardens. (Both photographs by Leet-Melbrook, Inc., M-NCPPC.)

On December 13, 1968, young residents get their first look at the new ice-skating rink being constructed by the Maryland-National Capital Park and Planning Commission in Wheaton Regional Park. They're ready to take to the ice, but, unfortunately, they will have to wait for opening day, which was set for Saturday, December 21. (M-NCPPC.)

Wheaton Ice Rink's top skaters completed their skating proficiency tests under the auspices of the Ice Skating Institute of America. From left to right are Nancy Edler, Freestyle I (12 and under); Leslie Kushner, Beta test; Artie Robbins, Freestyle I (12 and over); Linda Robbins, sportsmanship award; Carolyn Martin, Gamma test; Beverly Reese, Freestyle II; senior instructor Anne Rieley; and rink manager Greg Fuller. (M-NCPPC.)

Maryland's first arboretum opened in the summer of 1969 at a cost of $250,000 on 24 acres at the northern edge of Wheaton Regional Park. "A place where our residents can come to enjoy the beauty, to be in a quiet place of meditation, to think in an environment of noninterference," was the sentiment of one county official. Designed by Swiss-trained architect Hans E. Hanses, the construction took four years and included a 60-by-100-foot greenhouse featuring floral displays arranged beside a quiet clear brook, and formal rock and ornamental grass gardens were started in the acreage outside of the greenhouse. (Both M-NCPPC.)

The Athletic Area was advertised as an "active sports area for both participation and spectator events, with tennis, handball, baseball and softball facilities provided." Included were six ball fields (two lighted for night play). All ball field use was by permit only with "ample parking, bleachers for spectators, refreshment concession and locker room available." (Photograph by Leet-Melbrook, Inc., M-NCPPC.)

"Melanie, Meet Napoleon." A children's pony ring opened in the park, and one of the first visitors to the "ranch" was young Melanie Smith of Kensington, who is shown here with her dad, Jean Paul Smith. Napoleon was one of 13 residents at the pony ring who, for a 25¢ fare, let youngsters ride around the corral. (WKCC.)

Beginning in 1972, the Gude Garden was created as a memorial to Adolph Gude Sr. who was a prominent local nurseryman. M-NCPPC landscape architect Hans Hanses designed the Japanese-style landscape of soft rolling hills and the Japanese Teahouse overlooking the ponds. The teahouse is on an island planted with bamboo, conifers, and ground covers. The Gude family donated many of the specimen trees and shrubs, including the beech trees, blue Atlas cedars, southern magnolia, and most of the conifers on the island. The Kousa dogwood collection was added in 1991. Over the years, the ponds have become home to many species of wildlife and colorful Japanese koi donated from private collections. In 2004, a "contemplative place for healing and remembrance" was dedicated: the Reflection Terrace, located along the pond side in the Gude Garden, in remembrance of the 2002 sniper victims. (Both M-NCPPC.)

On May 19, 1985, the first county-owned carousel was dedicated. It was purchased for $60,000 from Eva and Jim Wells of Fairfax, Virginia, owner/operators of the carousel on the Mall near the Smithsonian Institution Castle. The motto of their company, Melody Farms, was "Our Business Is All Fun." They also rented Wurlitzer band organs and brought one to the festivities that day. The carousel is actually a mixture of Herschell-Spillman and Spillman Engineering figures built between 1910 and 1915. It has 33 jumping horses, 3 menagerie animals, and 2 chariots, but no band organ. Many of the Wellses' carousel figures were restored in the author's apartment in Virginia—in 10 animal deliveries. As part of an agreement signed when the Ovid Hazen Wells farm was deeded to the M-NCPPC, the carousel was temporarily placed in Wheaton until the Clarksburg park was built and would be returned when there were enough residents in the area to support it. It is scheduled to leave in 2015 and will be a great loss to the Wheaton community. (Above author; below M-NCPPC.)

The miniature train has been part of the park since it opened. A replica of an 1863 C. P. Huntington engine pulls the train on a 10-minute tour. The original Magruder homestead is behind the tracks. Passengers purchase a ticket and depart from the train station for a ride through forest and meadow, over a trestle bridge, and past Pine Lake. The train does not operate in inclement weather. (M-NCPPC.)

The National Capital Trolley Museum, formed as a nonprofit organization in 1959, is located on Bonifant Road. The M-NCPPC allowed the organization to develop the museum in Northwest Branch Regional Park with private funding. The museum dedicates itself to the history of streetcars, and part of the collection takes visitors on a trolley ride on the track around the grounds. (WKCC.)

Nine

COMMUNITY UNDER CONSTRUCTION

The *Commuter* seems an apt symbol for the Wheaton area. He is a cast-bronze sculpture frozen in time in the act of hurrying away from the Wheaton Metro. The sculpture was commissioned by the Montgomery County government as part of the Art in Public Architecture program in 1989 and dedicated in 1991. The artist, Marcia F. Billig, created a full-length figure of a man shod in four-wheeled roller skates hurrying away, wearing a suit, tie, and hat with a briefcase gripped in one hand and a newspaper in the other. One hopeful aspect is that the commuter caught up in a frantic pace can be imagined hurrying home rather than to work. (Author.)

In 1969, Anna Marcus wrote in the *Wheaton News* about the mixed emotions of those listening to the plans outlined in the Kensington-Wheaton Master Plan for a Metro, buried wires, sign control, and pedestrian walkways crossing Veirs Mill Road, Georgia Avenue, and even one over the water storage tanks where parking was projected to be built: "Probably none of us will be around when the Ultimate Wheaton arises, but as to our children perhaps they will see the fruits of plans that have been made, hashed and rehashed for years. . . . may all be satisfied when that time does

come!" This bird's-eye view of Wheaton taken in 2004 shows a few of these plans realized: the walkway across Veirs Mill Road and the Wheaton Metro. Westfield Wheaton has expanded and is now enclosed, and there are no more residents in the triangle. It is hard to imagine so much change could take place in only 60 years. (Photograph by Air Photos USA, Bozzuto Development Company, Loiederman Soltesz Associates, Inc.)

Located near the Wheaton Metro, Georgia Avenue (on left traveling north), and Reedie Drive, the mural *The Spirit of Wheaton* was designed and painted by students of the Maryland College of Art and Design. The artists were Mike Anthony, Roger Chavez, Kevin Denley, Sharon Hoover, Ginau Mathurin, and Tony Williams. A brass historical marker provides a key to the images depicted: Graeves Home, 1922; Lieshner Radio Repair, 1948; Little Tavern Cafe, 1950; Hickerson Station and Store, 1925; and Getty Farm, 1912. The mural, completed in 1990, was sponsored by Wheaton Urban District Committee, Wheaton and Kensington Chamber of Commerce, Keep Montgomery County Beautiful Task Force, and Montgomery County government. Only the Little Tavern still existed at that time, but it too is now gone. (Both author.)

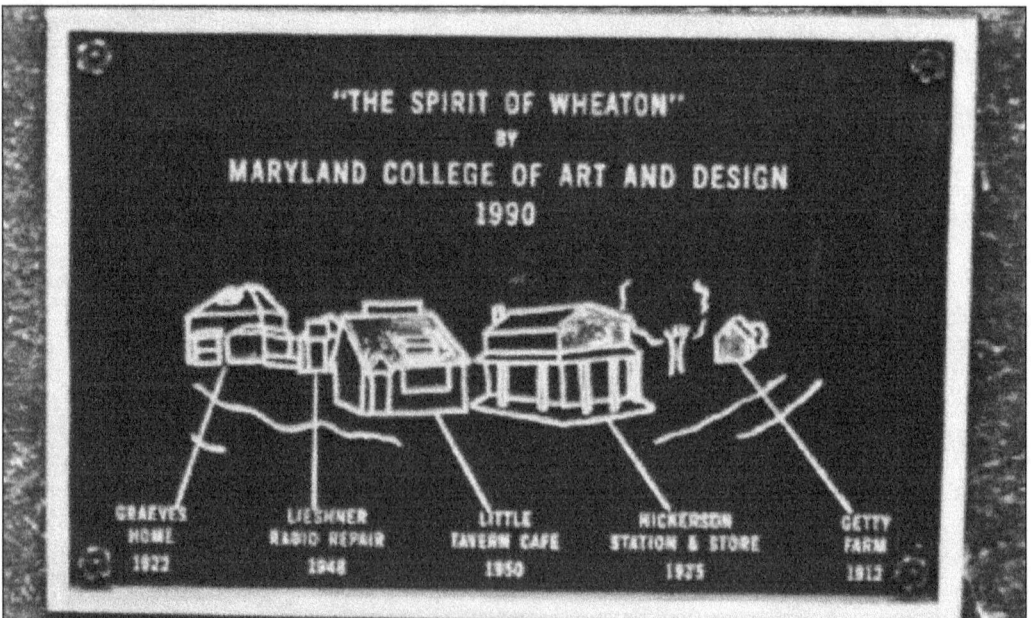

BIBLIOGRAPHY

Boyd, T. H. S. *The History of Montgomery County, Maryland, from it Earliest Settlement in 1650 to 1879.* Baltimore, MD: Regional Publishing Company, reprinted 1968.

Clarke, Nina H., and Lillian B. Brown. *History of the Black Public Schools of Montgomery County, Maryland, 1872–1961.* New York: Vantage Books, 1978.

www.dcrtv.com

Farquhar, Roger Brooke. *Historic Montgomery County, Maryland, Old Homes and History.* Silver Spring, MD: Monumental Printing Company, 1952.

"Kensington-Wheaton Guide." Special Issue, H. M. Flinn. 1952.

Gartrell, Joan. *Hughes United Methodist Church Dedication September 22, 1985.* Silver Spring, MD: Hughes United Methodist Church, 1985.

Getty, Mildred Newbold. "Wheaton: The Montgomery County Story." Rockville, MD: Montgomery County Historical Society, Vol. XIV November 1970, No. 1.

MacMaster, Richard K., and Ray Eldon Hiebert. *A Grateful Remembrance: The Story of Montgomery County, Maryland 1776–1976.* Rockville, MD: Montgomery County Government, 1996.

Maryland Geological Survey, *Highways of Maryland.* Baltimore, MD. John Hopkins Press, 1899.

———. *Highways of Maryland,* Vol. V. Baltimore, MD: John Hopkins Press, 1905.

www.RACampbell.com

Warfield, J. D. *The Founders of Anne Arundel and Howard Counties, Maryland.* Baltimore, MD: Regional Publishing, 1967.

Warner, Michael. *A Work in Progress: St. Catherine Labouré Parish 1951–2001.* Silver Spring, MD: St. Catherine Labouré, 2001.

www.widmarcs.com

www.williamfuld.com

www.wqmrwgaymemories.org

A NOTE TO THE READER:

Multiple naming for geographic locations, farms, businesses, and roads (especially roads) has a long history. In this text, after an earlier perhaps unfamiliar name is used, a parenthesis follows with the current name. Georgia Avenue has also been called Seventh Street Pike, Westminster Road, the Union Plank, Brookeville Pike, the Turnpike, the Union Plank, Union Turnpike, and the Brookeville and Washington Turnpike and quite possibly other names the author is unaware of. Wheaton has been known as Leesborough, the Cross Roads, Mitchell's Crossroads, Leesboro, and Mitchells X Roads.

Visit us at
arcadiapublishing.com